LAURA

Luxurious Chiang Mai
The Ultimate Travel Guide to Having a 5-Star Holiday or Honeymoon in Chiang Mai

By Laura Gibbs

Luxurious Chiang Mai by Laura Gibbs

Published © 2017 Laura Gibbs

All rights reserved. No portion of this book may be reproduced in any form without permission from the publisher. For permissions contact:

Thailandstoriesbook@gmail.com

'Take care of the luxuries and the necessities will take care of themselves.'

- Dorothy Parker

TABLE OF CONTENTS

Introduction 14

Hotels 15

137 Pillars House

Puripunn Baby Grand Boutique Hotel

Na Nirand Romantic Boutique Resort

Anantara Chiang Mai Resort

Villa Mahabhirom

Shangri La Hotel

Akyra Manor

Siripanna Villa Resort & Spa

Four Seasons Chiang Mai

Veranda High Resort

Rati Lanna Riverside Spa Resort

Oasis Baan Saen Doi Spa Resort

Panviman Spa Resort

Dhara Dhevi Chiang Mai

Ping Nakara Boutique hotel

Rachamanka

Le Meridien

Kantary Hills Hotel

Sireeampan Boutique Resort and Spa

Howie's Homestay

Airbnb

Sightseeing in Chiang Mai *49*

Doi Suthep

Doi Pui

Phuping Palace

Chedi Luang

Wat Phra Singh

Thapae Gate & The Fortress Wall

Silver temple

Wat Umong

Lanna Folklife Museum

Chiang Mai Historical Centre

Chiang Mai University

Wiang Kum Kam

Art in Paradise

Chiang Mai Night Safari

Queen Sirikit Botanical Garden

Chiang Mai Zoo

Activities *59*

Flight of the Gibbon Zipline

Elephant riding
- *Thai Elephant Conservation Center (TECC)*
- *Elephant Nature Park*

- *The Elephant Jungle Sanctuary*

Motorbiking

Monk chat

Hot air balloon

Yoga
- *Wild Rose Studio*
- *Thailand Yoga Holidays*

Cooking schools
- *The Chiang Mai Thai Cookery School*
- *May Kaidee's Cooking School*

Golf
- *Royal Chiang Mai*
- *North Hill City Resort*
- *Chiang Mai Highlands*
- *Chiangmai Inthanon Golf and Natural Resort*

Chiang Mai Nature *69*

Doi Pui viewpoints

Huey Kaew Waterfall

Grand Canyon

Huey Tung Tao

Bua Tong Waterfall

Doi Inthanon

Phra Chor Canyon

Mae Sa Valley

Mae Sa Waterfall

Mon Cham

Royal Flora Ratchaphruek

Art Galleries 76

- Thapae East
- Suvannabhumi Art Gallery
- Meeting Room Cafe
- Galerie Panisa
- Maiiam
- Gallery Seescape
- Wattana Art Gallery

Fine Dining 79

- Italics
- David's Kitchen
- Ginger & Kafe at The House
- Time at Na Nirand
- Farang Ses
- The Restaurant at Rachamankha
- Palette at 137 Pillars House
- China Kitchen
- Norden
- Allegro and Fujian
- Le Coq d'Or Restaurant
- Le Crystal
- The Service 1921
- Cuisine De Garden

Thai Cuisine 94

Try Thai in style
- *Le Grand Lanna*
- *Rim Tai Kitchen*
- *Slee Banyan at the Siripanna Resort*
- *Ruen Tamarind Restaurant*
- *Saenkham Terrace*
- *The River Market*

Traditional and Local Thai
- *Traditional Khantoke Dinner*
- *Tong Tem Teh*
- *Huen Phen*
- *Hot Chilli*
- *Dash*
- *Lemongrass Restaurant*

Street food
- *Chiang Mai gate*
- *Sunday Walking Street Market*
- *Ploen Rudee Night Market*

Cafes & High Tea 105

Doppio Ristr8to

Asama

Akha Ama

Woo Cafe and Gallery

Fabb Coffee Roasters

Tita Gallery

Dhara Dhevi Cake Shop

Anantara High Tea

137 Pillars High Tea

Nakara Jardin

Vieng Joom On

Punna Café

Bars / Nightlife *114*

North Gate Jazz Bar

Boys Blues Bar

Maya Rooftop

Rise Rooftop Bar

Yayee Rooftop Bar

Riverside Bar and Restaurant

Beer Lab

Mixology Bar

The Service 1921 Bar

Red Room Wine Bar

Warm Up

Infinity

UN Irish Pub

Shopping *121*

Markets
- *Sunday Walking Street*
- *Saturday Walking Street*
- *Warorot and the Ton Lamyai Flower Market*
- *Night Bazaar*

Antiques
- *The Golden Triangle*

- T. Tara Collection
- Nina Antiques

Handicrafts
- Bor Sang Village
- Handicraft Highway
- Ban Tawai

Clothing & textiles
- Studio Naenna
- Doi Tung Lifestyle
- Vila Cini
- WEAVE
- Ginger
- Mesimu

Jewellery
- Eranyara
- Nova Jewellery
- Metal Studio Thailand
- Royal Orchid Company

Other
- Herb Basics
- Gerard collection
- Crafitti
- Sop Moei Arts
- Shinawatra Thai Silk

Pampering and Spa Time..136

Anantara Spa

Panna Spa

The Spa at 137 Pillars House

Cheeva Spa

The Oasis Spa

Fah Lanna Spa

Kiyora Spa

Dheva Spa and Wellness Centre

Rarinjinda Wellness Spa

Where to next? Trips out of Chiang Mai **145**

Chiang Rai

Mae Sai & Golden Triangle

Doi Tung Royal Villa

Mae Fah Luang garden

Chiang Rai Resorts

Golden Triangle Elephant Camps
- *Anantara Chiang Rai*
- *Four Seasons Tented Camp*

Pai
- *Reverie Siam*
- *Pai Island Resort*
- *Montis Resort*

Chiang Dao
- *Chiang Dao Nest*
- *Azalea Village*

Mountain float

Sukhothai Historical Park

Events **157**

January
- *Bor Sang Umbrella Festival*
- *Chinese New Year*

Febuary
- *Chiang Mai Flower Festival*

- *Makha Bucha Day*
- *Strawberry Fair*

April
- *Songkran (Thai New Year)*

May
- *Wisakha Bucha Day*

November
- *Yee Ping*
- *Loy Kratong*

December
- *Christmas & New Year*

Practical Issues *164*

Weather

Visas

Airport Lounges

Medical and Safety Issues

Money

The end *168*

INTRODUCTION

After living in Thailand for five years I have become the 'go to' person for travel questions whenever friends, or friends of friends, visit Thailand. Since I have travelled extensively throughout the country, I welcome the chance to share my knowledge and wish to highlight some of the amazing places I have seen to other travellers. However I noticed a distinct gap of information when a honeymooning couple came to visit Chiang Mai. *Where should we stay? What should we do? Where do we find great Thai food? I can't eat Thai food, what other options are there? Which elephant camp is best? Most ethical?* The questions continued for days, but eventually the couple managed to arrange their dream holiday. After a few more discerning travellers were referred to me, all with similar questions, I decided to write a guide to finding luxury in Chiang Mai.

This guide covers the best hotels, restaurants, spas, activities, bars, cafes, shopping experiences and nature spots that Chiang Mai has to offer. While Chiang Mai is so often talked about as being cheap and a great spot for budget travellers, it is rarely mentioned as being one of the best places in the world for affordable five star luxury. With some of the most amazing resorts in the county, Chiang Mai should be a place to splurge even on a budget and enjoy the finer things in life. Sip a cocktail in a plunge pool overlooking rice fields. Stay in a tent with a freestanding bath tub, or in a colonial suite overlooking a replicated miniature kingdom. Explore majestic nature on jungle treks, or from your balcony, and visit the golden temple perched above a city. Meet and bathe rescued elephants, or indulge in a five hour pampering session. Chiang Mai offers everything to make your dreams come true.

After reading this guide, if you still have questions about your holiday, head over to www.luxurychiangmai.com where you can contact me directly. Happy holidays!

Laura Gibbs
Chiang Mai, Thailand
20/10/2016

HOTELS

Choosing the correct hotel is important for making your holiday unforgettable. From aesthetics to service, dining to activities, the luxury hotels in Chiang Mai have gone above and beyond to provide guests with a dream holiday they will never forget. Interestingly, Chiang Mai as a city has a low cost of living, and the hotels reflect this, offering unparalleled service at a fraction of the cost of other tourist cities in the world. So whether you soak up luxury on a daily basis, or this is your holiday of the year, the following hotels and resorts have been recognised time and again as the best hotels in Chiang Mai (and in Asia) and so will contribute to a truly unforgettable holiday experience - be it a vacation or a honeymoon.

Once you have found your base, it's time to explore! Chiang Mai boasts cooler temperatures than most parts of Thailand, as well as beautiful views of rice paddies and the green, rolling mountains of Doi Pui national park. From your chosen luxury hotel, visitors can discover the old city's many temples, local markets and ancient Lanna ruins. Thanks to foreign influence, there are many places to soak up the cosmopolitan vibe in unique cafés, boutiques and art galleries. Should you decide to venture further afield, you will discover native wildlife, river rafting experiences, dense tropical rainforest, hill tribes, and quaint handcrafted villages near Chiang Mai.

137 PILLARS HOUSE

The 137 Pillars House is considered a historical and luxurious masterpiece. The main structure of the hotel dates back to 1889, although it has since been refurbished to high historical standards by architects and local conservationists. The 137 Pillars House started life as the headquarters of the British Borneo Trading Company, before laying in ruins for many years. It was eventually re-discovered by a Thai family who decided to renovate and share the history of the house and the area with the world. Today the property features a museum on the ground floor and a living room, fit for high tea and meals, on the upper floor. The small, but spacious hotel has an onsite spa, two restaurants, swimming pool, as well as 30 immaculate suites, all well equipped to make your stay as comfortable and memorable as possible.

The 137 Pillars offers four historical room types. The Rajah Brooke suites feature a tiled veranda overlooking the gardens, separate indoor and outdoor showers, as well as a free standing Victorian bath to help guests unwind. Six East Borneo suites offer more space and even more refined decor. The spacious 100 sqm William Bain Terrace suites have their own living areas for added space, and are perfect for families who are looking for private areas to relax, while the two Louis Leonowens Pool Suites are the pinnacle rooms in this property. Each over 135 square metres, they feature their own private swimming pools and are spacious enough for guests to never leave their rooms (except for the elaborate daily breakfast buffet). The 137 Pillars House can also host weddings, social functions or meetings to impress, and offers various packages including a weekend getaway from Bangkok by private jet.

www.137pillarschiangmai.com
Address: 2 Soi 1, Nawatgate Road, Wat gate
Tel: +66 (0) 53 247 788
Email: info@137pillarshouse.com

Best for: Discerning travellers looking for the finest quality rooms, and wishing explore the history of Chiang Mai

PURIPUNN BABY GRAND BOUTIQUE HOTEL

An intimate hotel with just 30 rooms, Puripunn Baby Grand Boutique Hotel is compact, well designed and worthy of calling itself a luxury boutique hotel. Puripunn Baby Grand has been designed in a mixture of traditional Lanna and Thai architecture with small finishing touches that can be seen everywhere. The hallways and balconies are tiled with bright patterns, while the main entrance hall is elaborate and welcoming. The staff are all dressed in traditional clothing, adding to the atmosphere, and they are extremely helpful in the attempt to make your holiday the best possible. Upon arrival you immediately experience Thai hospitality, with an offering of a welcome drink and iced towel to wash away the outside stress. You are then led to your room to relax and recuperate in a mixture of Lanna and colonial interior with fresh flowers adding the finishing touches to the rooms.

The Superior rooms are spacious and well-designed containing a writing desk, sofa and tv unit. The bathroom features a beautiful sink and a bathtub, while the outdoor balconies offer pool and garden views. Puripunn Deluxe rooms on the ground floor each have a private terrace enclosed with tropical plants and an outdoor daybed. The deluxe has an impressive bathroom with a bathtub, bathroom sofa and a separate rain shower room, great for those who spend lots of time pampering themselves. The single Puripunn Grand Suite has its own private pool as well as a separate living area, Jacuzzi bathtub and dual wash basins for him and her. The Grand Suite is spacious and decorated in a regal olive green, with dark wooden floors and a four poster bed. The two Baby suites feature elegant décor in hushed colours, a separate spacious living area and a veranda with a daybed. Choose from the Baby Suite with a Jacuzzi bathtub or a vintage freestanding bathtub to soak away your troubles and return to a state of relaxation.

As well as your room, the pool area is a great place to relax, either in the daytime shaded by the tropical trees or at night when the trees are dressed in fairy lights. The café and restaurant area offers delicious food all day, from the complimentary breakfast buffet to a range of traditional dishes from lunch and dinner. Small and charming, Puripunn Baby Grand hotel is not to be missed for those looking to experience a small slice of tradition, culture and beauty.

www.puripunn.com
Address: 104/1 Charoen Muang Road, Soi 2, Wat Gate
Tel: +66 (0) 53 302 898
Email: rsvn@puripunn.com

Best for: Travellers looking for a touch of Thai life

NA NIRAND ROMANTIC BOUTIQUE RESORT

The most impressive feature of Na Nirand Romantic Boutique Resort has to be the magnificent 100 year old rain tree. The legend says Mr. H Slade, the first conservator and founder of Chiang Mai's conservation department, planted the tree, and today it stands in a prime position to be admired by guests while relaxing in luxury. The tree is the heart of Na Nirand, which in Thai means timeless elegance, and the hotel breathes its meaning effortlessly. From arrival to departure, this property welcomes guests and allows them to slow down and find their natural rhythm. The resort has combined a mixture of traditional Thai Lanna and colonial architecture, making use of the small space to ensure the privacy and peacefulness of each guest. With a delicious restaurant, small spa, library, private conference room and riverside views on site, there is no reason to leave Na Nirand. If you do go to explore Chiang Mai, then upon return you are met with the impressive grandfather raintree, impossible not to admire.

Na Nirand has 45 rooms but at no point does the resort feel crowded, or even inhabited. The design of the property allows guests complete privacy and a chance to relax by the river. The Romantic Lanna Deluxe rooms come in 3 different styles and are all decorated with local rattan furniture and handicrafts from Chiang Mai artisans. Each room is unique with different headboards and traditional Lanna hand woven art on the walls. The bathrooms and balconies feature colonial tiles and the beds are the height of comfort. The Romantic Lanna Grand Deluxe rooms offer more space and a living area, for those looking to relax inside. The Romantic Lanna Royal Deluxes have free standing baths for those who enjoy pampering themselves. The two corner suites offer wooden eaves and a classic elegance to the dark wood furnishings, and their balconies offer perfect views of the giant rain tree and the Ping river. Finally for those looking for the best, the House of Colonial offers four uniquely designed luxury suites. Each with a spacious living area with ornately decorated furniture and a large, sophisticated bathroom, these suites share a private infinity pool on their doorstep and exceptional river views.

www.nanirand.com
Address: 1/1 Soi 9, Charoenprathet Road, Chang Klan
Tel: +66 (0)53 280 988
Email: rsvn@nanirand.com

Best for: Romantic getaways and marriage proposals

ANANTARA CHIANG MAI RESORT

Situated along the edge of the Mae Ping River and located in the centre of the city of Chiang Mai, the Anantara Resort is a tropical and tranquil sanctuary. A mixture of colonial and contemporary zen style, the resort has catered for everything guests might want or need, taking all the stress out of travelling. Upon arrival guests are given a welcome drink, snack and floral necklace, followed by a five minute complimentary shoulder massage to bring visitors into a state of relaxation. The main feature of the Anantara Chiang Mai is the first British consulate building, which has been restored into The Service 1921 restaurant. The grounds offer a riverside pool, an exclusive spa, gym, meeting room and regular cultural events such as Thai boxing, cooking and Thai massage courses, as well as excursions to temples and local markets. There is also a nightly show of traditional Lanna music and dancing outside the old consulate building. The Anantara Chiang Mai is most well known for its afternoon tea, but guests can also have an extraordinary Peruvian dinner on the waterfront deck or even in the secret room hidden behind a bookcase.

The Anantara Chiang Mai has 84 rooms in total, encircling the grounds in a modern building made of glass and wood. Each room has its own private balcony complete with daybed and beautiful views over the river. All the rooms feature an entrance lobby to change your shoes for slippers, and to leave the stress of outside behind. The rooms are decorated in wood and have countless thoughtful extras, from yoga mats to daily seasonal fruit. The bathrooms are fitted with deep terrazzo tubs, rain showers and collapsible walls. The Kasara suites boast double the space of the Deluxe rooms and are perfect for couples desiring accommodation with more space and luxury, as well as families with up to two children. Across the road from the Anantara are 27 serviced one, two and three bedroom suites decorated in elegant Thai homely designs, and featuring two kitchens - one indoor western style, and one outdoor Thai style kitchen. The rooftop offers an infinity pool with mountain and river views, and for anyone hosting a party or wedding, this secret spot is stunning.

www.chiang-mai.anantara.com
Address: 123-123/1 Charoen Prathet Road, Chang Klan
Tel: +66 (0) 53 253 333
Email: chiangmai@anantara.com

Best for: Active travellers who want to experience everything Chiang Mai has to offer.

VILLA MAHABHIROM

A private and secluded getaway at the foot of the mountain, Villa Mahabhirom offers 14 traditional Thai style villas, a salt water plunge pool and one of the most unique hotel stays in Chiang Mai. Opened at the start of 2017 Villa Mahabhirom took seven years to design, craft and perfect, and the result is a is a luxurious property that highlights the traditional way of Thai life and celebrates the fine craftsmanship of Thai architecture.

Villa Mahabhirom is a small boutique hotel with a mixture of one, two or three bedroom villas as well as a separate three bedroom complex with a private pool. The villas, and the hotel itself are the epitome of luxury and calm, and nature agrees. Local species of birds have made Villa Mahabhirom their home, singing and dancing among the frangipani trees in the daytime. The rooms offer a chance to stay in a high end version of traditional houses, with almost all of the original features kept but updated to fit even the most discerning guest. Next to the wooden bedrooms are immaculate marble bathrooms with large free standing bathtubs, spacious showers and fluffy white towels.

The hotel grounds are compact but feel spacious, and offer countless interesting and original artistic pieces. The clean, zen areas of the hallways feel more like walking in an art gallery than a hotel. There is a library area with a balcony overlooking the pool as well as a café area offering views of the property from above. There is also indoor and outdoor dining areas, or the option to have your breakfast poolside. The small winding street Villa Mahabhirom sits on offers access to Wat Umong (a serene forest temple), quirky cafes and countless local artist studios, and within 15 minutes you will can access Chiang Mai's old city. Villa Mahabhirom is the perfect escape from city life, and a chance to explore traditional Thai culture in a luxurious way.

www.villamahabhirom.com
Address: 62 Moo. 10 Tambon Suthep, A. Muang Chiang Mai 50200
Tel: (+66) 053.271.200
Email: reserve@villamahabhirom.com

Best for: Art lovers and the most discerning of travellers

SHANGRI LA HOTEL

A classic 5 star hotel with elegance and sophistication, the Shangri La Hotel in Chiang Mai is a good option for those looking for luxury. Rooms at the Shangri La Hotel have an understated classic look with cream walls, peach and cherry coloured cushions, and teak wood furniture. Located in a quiet part of town and very close to the old city and night bazaar, the Shangri La hotel is perfect for those looking to spend more time in the hotel and avoid busy Chiang Mai. The hotel has a beautiful pool with private lounging day beds, a sauna and a steam room, tennis courts, a fully equipped fitness centre and the CHI spa, which includes large private suites and offers many Asian healing treatments.

Each room in the Shangri-La Hotel is furnished to a high standard of quality with rain showers, a small lounge area and vast city or mountain views. However, the suites are more spacious, some with kitchens and dining areas for those who wish to try out their newly acquired Thai culinary skills. The Presidential suite is a five bay, 215 square metre suite on the top floor, decorated in Lanna renaissance style. It features a 10 person dining table and is perfect for business travellers or wedding parties.

www.shangri-la.com/chiangmai/shangrila/
Address: 89/8 Chang Klan Road
Tel:+66 (0) 53 253 888
Email: slcm@shangri-la.com

Best for: Elegance lovers

LUXURIOUS CHIANG MAI

AKYRA MANOR

One of the most centrally located luxury hotels and with only 30 rooms, the Akyra Manor is a great mix of architecture, luxury and modern style. The Akyra Manor is part of the visionary and innovative AKARYN Hotel Group, hailing from Singapore, so it's no wonder that this hotel is fit for any modern city. The building has an interesting exterior that's meant to represent the outside coming in. Meanwhile inside, the décor is mostly stylish shades of black and silver, a cooling contrast to the bright and busy world outside.

The compact reception on the ground floor is part of the popular Italics restaurant, so guests don't even need to venture outside to find great food. On each of the eight floors the walls are lined with satin curtains, and there is artwork from a local artist showcased next to the elevator on each floor. Both in the corridors and the rooms the Akyra playlist playing soothingly in the background; a combination of chilled and soulful music that has been selected for day or night can be heard throughout the hotel. The music is one of countless small touches that add to guest's wellbeing. Plugs that can still charge even if the power is off in the room, the ingredients of a daily cocktail carefully placed in your room, a pillow menu, his and her drawers of useful complementary items in the bathroom, a modern coffee machine and even a traditional night time drink placed on bedside tables to help guests relax into the plush beds for a great night's sleep. Then there is the freestanding round bathtub with great views of the mountain that sits in the middle of each room: the list goes on. The Manor suites have an additional lounge room to almost double the room size and bring space into your stay.

LUXURIOUS CHIANG MAI

The Akyra Manor would fit both young professionals looking to experience as much of Chiang Mai as possible, families who love excitement and adventure, as well as those who prefer city life and a faster pace. The whole city is a stone's throw away from the Akyra Manor and on the rooftop Rise bar with stunning views and ostentatious drinks to entertain anyone. There are bicycles for rent from reception and the staff can assist guests to book different tours, yoga classes within the hotel, temple or elephant visits, ziplining and even a half day fishing course. If you are lucky enough to secure one of Akyra Manors 30 rooms then the added touches and helpful staff will make sure you have an amazing stay.

www.theakyra.com/chiang-mai/
Address: 22/2 Nimmanhaemin Road, Soi 9
Tel: +66 (0) 2 514 8112
Email: rsvn.akmc@theakyra.com

Best for: Young professionals and city lovers

SIRIPANNA VILLA RESORT & SPA

A beautiful, spacious resort with rooms and villas lining a large square pool with an island of frangipani trees in its centre, The Siripanna Villa resort offers 104 rooms decorated in Lanna style. Choose from deluxe rooms with garden areas or gallery suites with large balconies overlooking the rice fields and art commissioned by local Lanna artists. The Siripanna grand royal Lanna suite is the ultimate in relaxing luxury, with a private living room, rooftop garden Jacuzzi, balcony and private pavilion. The Royal Lanna villas circle the swimming pool and is perfect for anyone wishing to swim in the mornings.

The Siripanna Villa Resort also has its own spa located within the hotel, as well as a traditional Thai house available for art and cultural events. The house is a great space for weddings or social gatherings and a cooking studio is also attached, which offers guests the chance to learn some of the complexities of Thai culinary skills with their own personal chef. Rice fields and gardens containing seasonal fruits and vegetables are located at the rear of the resort, and guests can try their hand at rice harvesting or planting depending on the season, as well as exploring the gardens and picking some ripe tropical fruit right off the trees. Throughout the resort's manicured gardens visitors can get a glimpse of rare South East Asian flowers and fauna unique to this region.

www.siripanna.com
Address: 36 Rat Uthit Road, Tambon Wat Ket
Tel: +66 (0) 5329 4656
E-mail: info@siripanna.com

Best for: Families and those wishing to explore Thai life

FOUR SEASONS CHIANG MAI

The Four Seasons is another spectacular luxury hotel in Chiang Mai. A 20-minute drive away from Chiang Mai city, the Four Seasons is nestled in the Mae Rim Valley and surrounded by mountains and lush rainforest. The Resort is encircled by rice paddies and an infinity pool, and offers cool temperatures, fresh air and some of the most well-appointed suites in Thailand. The model of the Four Seasons was copied in creating the Dhara Dhevi, and while the Dhara Dhevi hotel is unique in its own right, the Four Seasons retains its reserved dignity and timeless style. For keen adventurers as well as those in need of a hideaway or relaxation, this is the perfect hotel.

The Four Seasons offers a variety of pavilions, all of which have verandas perched above the sprawling grounds, decorated with polished teak wood flooring, rich Thai silk decorations and beautiful Siamese art, all under a vaulted ceiling with cooling overhead fans. The pool villas are surrounded by water on three sides and are the perfect choice for couples who desire total privacy, aquatic luxury, and a sense of immense flowing spaces, including an outdoor Thai sala pavilion.

The Four Seasons Chiang Mai also offer private residences located at the top of the property that provide a sense of space and offer spectacular views. With a capacity for up to 9 adults, the residences have a combination of sitting rooms, private pavilions and terraces with views of the surrounding landscape . The Penthouse bedroom residence features master bedrooms with private individual Jacuzzis. The interiors are fitted with all necessary modern amenities, penthouse terraces and thoughtfully decorated with chosen pieces that reflect authentic Thai art and craftsmanship. Finally, for those organising a wedding or event of a lifetime, a luxurious 20-bedroom private resort experience is also available.

www.fourseasons.com/chiangmai/
Address: Four Seasons Resort Chiang Mai , 502 Moo 1, Mae Rim-Samoeng Old Road
Telephone: +66 (0) 53 298 181

Best for: Nature lovers and getting away from it all

VERANDA HIGH RESORT

The Veranda High Resort is located 30 minutes outside of Chiang Mai city and perfect for those looking to avoid city life and be surrounded by nature and local Thai life on their holiday. Situated at the bottom of the impressive Doi Pui mountain range, one of the Veranda Resort's most impressive features is its infinity pool overlooking the rolling hills of northern Thailand, it serves as a perfect place to watch the sunset. There are impressive views throughout the resort, as well as fresher, cooler air and a wide range of exotic local birds. Since the resort is outside of the city, it is also the perfect place to stargaze at night.

The rooms at Veranda have been decorated in a modern zen style, with clean, crisp lines and wood to bring nature into the rooms. There are a total of 80 rooms that either focus on contemporary style or the cultural heritage of the region. From a compact comfy studio to two bedroom suites or the Presidential Pool Villa, Veranda offers a range of different room styles to suit your needs. The resort sits on the Samoeng loop, and is perfect for those who enjoy motor biking or cycling, as some of the best roads are easily accessible from Veranda High Resort.

www.verandaresortandspa.com
Address: 192 Moo 2 Banpong, Hang Dong
Tel: +66 (0) 53 365 007
E-mail: rsvn-chiangmai@verandaresort.com

Best for: Exploring Thailand's nature and lazing by the pool

LUXURIOUS CHIANG MAI

RATI LANNA RIVERSIDE SPA RESORT

The Rati Lanna Riverside Spa Resort is a boutique hotel sitting on the banks of the Mae Ping River with an authentic Northern Thai and Lanna style feel to it. From fresh flower displays and delicious Thai dinners overlooking the peaceful riverside, to relaxing spa treatments, Rati Lanna tries to make your stay as memorable and stress-free as possible. With 75 rooms and ample space, the resort never feels too busy and with four different dining options, an onsite cooking school, a large spa and an infinity pool, there is always something to do at Rati Lanna.

The elegant rooms at Rati Lanna continue to display traditional Thai décor, mixed with modernity. Bathrooms include rain showers as well as flat screen TVs mounted near the bathtubs. The deluxe suites are 120 square metres and feature private balconies, Jacuzzis, and separate bedroom and living room areas. The Riverside Garden Suite is an impressive 320 square meters and comes with its own balcony and gazebo, private plunge pool, indoor Jacuzzi, an outdoor dining area, treadmill, living room and home theatre system.

www.ratilannachiangmai.com
Address: 33 Changklan Road, Chang Klan
Tel.+66 (0) 53 999 333
Email : info@ratilannachiangmai.com

Best for: immersing in Thai culture

OASIS BAAN SAEN DOI SPA RESORT

Oasis Baan Saen Doi Spa Resort was born out of one of the most reputable spas in Chiang Mai: The Oasis Spa group. Their resort is a blend of luxury, relaxation and tropical escape, nestled 20 minutes south of Chiang Mai in the foothills of the Doi Pui mountain range. The resort doubles as a day spa and is perfect for guests who are looking for a taste of Thai and Lanna style massage and health treatments.

The rooms at the resort are finely decorated with traditional Lanna style fabrics and polished teakwood, and all feature relaxing views of the spas tropical gardens. The Luxury Suite is 75 square meters and is decorated with tribal art, a large bathroom with a rain shower and a Jacuzzi. The largest room is the Presidential Pool Villa, often booked out for ambassadors, and is a three-bedroom villa with a kitchen, private pool, dining room, and even outdoor showers. If you are looking for a romantic or pampering vacation, then consider Oasis Baan Saen Doi Spa Resort as a 'get away from it all' kind of place.

www.oasisluxury.net
Address: 199/135 Moo 3 Chonpratan Road, Mae Hia
Tel: +66 (0) 53 920 199
Email: cs@oasisluxury.net

Best for: Those who love to be pampered

PANVIMAN SPA RESORT

The Panviman Spa Resort is nestled deep in the Mae Sa Valley, 30 minutes north of Chiang Mai city. Surrounded by mountains and perched high on a mountainside this resort offers stunning views over the natural rainforest. It's not easy to find the resort but the traditional Thai design and facilities at the Panviman are impressive, and being hidden away adds to the allure. Most rooms as well as the restaurant offers stunning views over the valley and the three tier infinity pool is reason alone to stay at this resort.

The resort is located along the Samoeng loop and is perfect for motorbike enthusiasts and cyclists. For those who wish to remain inside the resort, there are lots of activities, including cooking classes, a library, fitness centre and yoga studio, mini golf course, jogging track, a games room, meditation cave and archery area. All the rooms at the Panviman Resort include private balconies with daybeds and stunning views. The Deluxe Rooms feature bathtubs and sitting areas, while the 7 Steam Villas and 7 Jacuzzi Villas have their own private facilities. The four exclusive Viman Pool Villas have their own private infinity pool attached to the balcony area and offers unparralelled views of the green rainforest.

www.panviman.com
Address: 197/2 Moo 1, Pongyang, highway 1096, Mae Rim
Tel : +66 (0) 5387 9540-5
E-mail: rsvn_chiangmai@panviman.com

Best for: Nature lovers who want to admire the mountain scenery

DHARA DHEVI CHIANG MAI

Formerly the Mandarin Oriental hotel, the renamed Dhara Dhevi was voted one of the world's best hotels by Travel + Leisure magazine in 2014. The hotel has been modeled into a miniature Thai kingdom focusing on detail and design, as well as recreating traditional architecture. Upon entering the hotel, guests are driven across a creaky wooden bridge, a traditional way of knowing guests are arriving into a kingdom. Guests then enter the hotel though a representation of a traditional Lanna gate.

The Dhara Dhevi spans over 60 acres of beautifully landscaped grounds and includes a historical theatre for weddings and events, novel rice fields with buffalo, a cultural centre, tennis courts, an Oriental Culinary Academy and nine different on site restaurants. The Dhara Dhevi hotel has varying accommodation options, from colonial suites with lounges and bathtubs, to two story Lanna inspired Villas complete with private pools. There is also a luxurious spa and wellness centre offering herbal treatments, massages, and an Ayurveda therapy program that can last from three hours up to 21 therapeutic days.

www.dharadhevi.com
Address: 51/4 Moo 1, Chiang Mai-Sankampaeng Road
Tel: +66 (0) 53 888 888
Email:enquiry@dharadhevi.com

Best for: travellers who wish to surround themselves in the ultimate luxurious setting

LUXURIOUS CHIANG MAI

PING NAKARA BOUTIQUE HOTEL

A beautiful, elaborate colonial building, the Ping Nakara Boutique hotel looks like a dream. The hotel reflects the past of Chiang Mai with a teak and colonial exterior. The gingerbread architecture, which is uncommon in Thailand, makes for a beautiful exterior and the style continues into the hotel. Upon entering guests are wowed with the lobby's tiled floor, floral decoration and beautiful Lanna style tapestry hanging on the wall. The elegance continues as you enter the outdoor courtyard, with a rich blue swimming pool, restaurant and indoor café and library. The courtyard is as beautiful as the exterior and a great place to relax or have an early dinner – there is even the option to have high tea in the courtyard.

The rooms at Ping Nakara each have their own design with unique hand crafted furniture and art. The rooms fit the romantic getaway style of Ping Nakara perfectly and are each named after Thai flowers. Of the 19 rooms, there are three different types; the Deluxe, the Grand Deluxe and the Royal Grand Deluxe. All the rooms are elegant and peaceful, with finely crafted extras that add to the experience. The Deluxe rooms don't have balconies and so are good for families. The rooms are just as elegant as the Grand Deluxe room, which have balconies overlooking the courtyard. All the rooms have separate bathtubs and showers, with the toiletries in the hotel rooms sourced from the spa. There are six Royal Grand Deluxe rooms, each offering a spacious bedroom, Jacuzzi tub, retro sofa and pool views from the balcony. As well as the hotel, Ping Nakara also has a spa attached to the hotel, which is available to outside visitors. Next door to the hotel is Nakara Jardin, a popular spot for high tea in a tranquil garden by the river.

www.pingnakara.com
Address: 135/9 Charoenprathet Road, Chang Klan
Tel: (66) 053 252 999
Email: info@pingnakara.com

Best for: Romantic getaways and couple retreats

RACHAMANKA

Rachamanka hotel is located just around the corner from one of Chiang Mai's most famous temples, Wat Phra Singh, and a two-minute walk to the famous Sunday Night Walking street. The hotel is relatively hidden from the street and its entrance does not show the whole expanse of the boutique hotel or its 20-metre pool. The Rachamanka commands a sense of peace and sophistication as guests pass through the courtyard into a walled sanctuary. Designed by Thai architect Ong-ard Satrabhandhu in the style of residential living to encourage a genuine feel for the history and culture of Lanna in Chiang Mai. The corridors display Thai antiques from different centuries and every room is uniquely decorated. Lovers of art and culture will appreciate the added details.

Rachamanka also has a library housing over 2,000 books, and 24 guest rooms showcasing Chinese furniture and original Asian art. Many are cherished objects from the owner's private collection, including rare scriptures and illustrated leaves from Buddhist tales, as well as contemporary abstract works from famous artists.

www.rachamankha.com
Address: 6 Rachamankha Road, soi 9, Phra Singh
Tel: +66 (0) 53 904 111
Email: contact@rachamankha.com

Best for: Culture lovers, and being in the heart of the city

LE MERIDIEN

Ideal for business travelers, younger couples and those who want comfort and quality without all the added decoration, then Le Meridien is a good place to stay. Right in the heart of the city, a stone's throw from the Night Bazaar and located along the main party street – Loi Kroh Road – the hotel has 383 rooms, with great city and mountain views. Another attraction of the Le Meridien is their large outdoor pool, ideal for watching sunset or sunbathing. Within the hotel there is a large meeting room complex, and the space can also be used for weddings, with the pool area converted into a tropical reception. On the ground floor is a fashionable Italian restaurant called Favola, Latitude 18 Bar for daytime and evening drinks or snacks, and on Sundays from 11:30-15:00 is one of the city's most popular brunches, offering a great range of buffet options as well as indoor and outdoor seating.

There are nine different room types to choose from so whatever you need can be catered for. The Deluxe and Urban rooms are simple, elegant and decorated all in white, from bathtub to the walls. The Urban rooms come with either city or Doi Suthep views, while the Escape rooms offer more space and views of the mountain also.

www.lemeridienchiangmai.com
Address: 108 Chang Klan Road, Chang Klan
Tel: +66 (0) 53 253 666
Email: reservations.chiangmai@lemeridien.com

Best for: Business and younger travellers looking for nightlife.

KANTARY HILLS HOTEL

A relatively unknown hotel chain, but this is where Thailand's Princess stays when she visits Chiang Mai. Located on a quiet street just off the trendy Nimmanhaemin Road, Kantary Hills offers both city and mountain views, as well as the luxury a Royal family member expects. Its location is convenient for both business travellers and explorers, as all areas of Chiang Mai are easy to access. It is also good for those who love shopping or city life, as the Nimmanhaemin area is packed with boutiques, restaurants and bars.

There are three different room varieties: Studio suites, one bedroom suites and two bedroom suites, all tastefully decorated in a contemporary style with walk in showers, bathtubs, kitchenettes, and all the necessary luxuries. If you are thinking about staying in Chiang Mai for a longer period of time, Kantary Hills also offers serviced apartments. Enclosed in the hotel is an outdoor swimming pool complete with a whirlpool, a reading room with complimentary tea and coffee, fitness centre, and a sauna and steam room. Kantary Hills also has an on-site limousine service if you want to travel in real style.

www.kantarygroup.com/kantaryhills-chiangmai/
Address: 44 Nimmanhaemin Road, Soi 12, Suthep
Tel: +66 (0) 53 22 2111
E-mail: reservations@kantaryhills-chiangmai.com

Best for: Royalty and those looking for privacy

SIREEAMPAN BOUTIQUE RESORT AND SPA

A small and relatively unknown 5 star hotel in Chiang Mai, Sireeampan Boutique Resort focuses more on quality than quantity. Hidden away in the foothills of Doi Pui Mountain, this peaceful area allows guests to relax and unwind in their own secluded sanctuary. Each one of the 11 suites (decorated with the feel of a luxurious Siamese heritage) has a different theme and colour attached to it, representing different gemstones. The S Class Studios are more spacious than the traditional studios, although both come with five fixture bathrooms complete with rain showers and standing bathtubs. The larger suites each have a separate living area and the S Class Suite also has an additional outdoor area. The suites are ideal for those who don't plan on leaving the hotel and want to relax in luxury. The Sireeampan Boutique Resort offers everything a guest might need to relax and recuperate - a 24 hour fitness centre and swimming pool, a spa with steam and sauna rooms, a menu of various therapeutic massages and treatments, and a complementary karaoke lounge to unwind and complete your de-stress. Meanwhile there is also a business lounge with two iMacs and coffee to create an office away from home.

www.sireeampan.com
Location:88/8 Moo 1, Chang Puak
Tel +66 (0)53 327 777
Email info@sireeampan.com

Best for: Privacy and work trips

HOWIE'S HOMESTAY

For travellers looking for a glimpse into what expat life in Thailand could look like, and for those looking to really get off the beaten track, Howie's Homestay is the perfect retreat. Neatly settled into the Mae Rim mountains, and a stone's throw away from the Four Seasons Resort, Howie's Homestay is a privately owned and custom designed villa by renowned architect Bill Bensley. The Thai- Lanna style of the villas and the centrepiece swimming pool with spectacular mountain views, is hugged by a sprawling lily pond, year round flowering gardens and open air pavilions for dining or relaxing.

Years ago Howie visited one of Richard Branson's open stay homes and although found the experience enjoyable, he felt that guests lacked complete privacy. He decided to open his tropical paradise home to outside travellers but with an added difference - your booking will ensure you are the only guests. Howie and his wife Jerri focus on exclusivity, privacy and one of a kind experiences for guests. From poolside massages, intimate honeymoon gatherings, trips into the jungle with elephants or even work meetings in the small amphitheatre, Howie can help curate your dream trip. When booking at Howie's Homestay the rates are fully inclusive of airport transfers, all meals and drinks, so prepare yourself for a feast! Jerri is an expert chef and every dinner creates eight different Thai dishes catered to guest's tastes. They even boast that if you stay a month you will never be offered the same dish twice - unless you request it. If you are a keen chef then there is a lot to be learned from Jerri and her alluring kitchen.

The villa rooms at the homestay are kitted out with the finest accessories, antiques and handicrafts, so wandering around Howie's home feels a lot like wandering through a museum. It is likely that Howie will even walk you through his palace himself and offer tips on the best places to go shopping in Chiang Mai. While he recommends his on call tour guide, a dinner with Howie and Jerri is where you are likely to learn all of Chiang Mai's secrets.

www.howieshomestay.com
Address: 78/1 Moo 1, Ban Mai, Mae Rim
Email: howie@howieshomestay.com
Tel: +66 081 882 8345

Best for: Luxury lovers looking for a friend in paradise

AIRBNB

As well as booking a hotel in Chiang Mai, it might be worth checking your dates on www.airbnb.com, as there are some amazing rentals in both the city centre of Chiang Mai as well as the surrounding area. For example, this giant *Charming Rustic Golden Teak Palace* costs around $300 a night and sleeps up to 12 people. Or a four bedroom spa villa with pool that can accommodate up to 12 people for around $500 per night.

If you are new to Airbnb then click this link for free travel credit when you book your first trip with Airbnb: www.airbnb.com/c/laurac347

SIGHTSEEING IN CHIANG MAI

Chiang Mai is one of the cultural gems of Southeast Asia and many people who visit the northern capital fall in love with its pace of life, the cultural heritage dotted all over the city, its easy access to nature and wide variety of amazing food and daytime activities. One week is a good amount of time to explore Chiang Mai and the outskirts, but prepare to be hooked and start planning your next trip back before you finish your first one!

Chiang Mai has a long and rich history that can be seen all over the city. Founded in 1296 by King Mengrai, Chiang Mai was the capital of the Lanna Kingdom (the Kingdom of a million rice fields) and served as the main trading town between southern China and the ports of Myanmar. The Kingdom covered most of northern Thailand as well as parts of Myanmar, China and Laos. Because of its strategic location, it was often attacked by its neighbours, yet for many years the old fortress walls of Chiang Mai kept attackers out. In 1557, Chiang Mai was successfully invaded by the Burmese and over the next 200 years it was fought over by the ruling Burmese kings as well as the Kingdom of Siam in the south. Eventually a partnership with the Kingdom of Siam, who was also struggling with Burmese invaders, led to Chiang Mai being recaptured by a Lanna King and in 1892 was peacefully incorporated into Siam. The Lanna Kingdom was condensed to a region around Chiang Mai, and in 1932 the area finally became a province of Siam, which later became known as Thailand.

Most local residents identify more with being from the Lanna kingdom than Thailand, still speak the traditional Lanna dialect and wear Lanna style clothes. After a few days in Chiang Mai, you might start to notice the difference between the two different styles and cultures. All over the city there are temples and ancient ruins offering a glimpse into the history and the Buddhist culture of Chiang Mai, but the pinnacle of the city's sightseeing is by far the golden temple resting on Chiang Mai's beautiful mountain.

DOI SUTHEP

Possibly the most famous temple in Thailand (after the King's Grand Palace complex in Bangkok) and definitely the most visited, the magnificent Wat Phra That Doi Suthep (Or Wat Doi Suthep for short) sits on the top of a mountain overlooking Chiang Mai city. The temple is deeply imbedded into Lanna culture and gives an example of the grandeur of the Kingdom in its prime. Legend says Wat Doi Suthep was founded on the spot where an ancient white elephant died while making a journey to Chiang Mai. The temple's origins date back to 1382 and is famous throughout the Buddhist region of Asia.

The journey up the winding mountain road is an experience in itself; for motorbike lovers it is a popular road to ride, for others a hired taxi lets you admire the glimpses of city and the dense virgin rainforest lining the road. No matter how you travel up to Doi Suthep, the final part of the journey to the temple is by 309 steps up a Naga (water serpent) lined staircase. The walk is worth it both for the views over Chiang Mai city, as well as to see the 600-year-old Chedi at the top. It is rumoured that the equivalent of over a million US Dollars is donated to the temple yearly, and visitors can glimpse the wealth from the sheer amount of gold visible on the Chedi. On the four corners of the Chedi are ceremonial parasols dating back to the 16th century and pilgrims make merit by sticking gold leafs to the corners while they circle the Chedi three times. Murals around the inner walls depict Buddhist teachings and historical events all the way back to Buddha's enlightenment. When you enter the temple complex there is a large Bodhi tree, also known as the Tree of Enlightenment. Around the outer walls of the temples are sets of Rakhang (temple bells) which are struck lightly by devout Buddhists (and visitors) to bring good luck.

Towards the back of the temple is a viewing platform offering stunning city views and, on clear days, views of the mountains surrounding Chiang Mai's valley. If you are interested in learning more about the meaning and practices of Buddhism then attached to Wat Doi Suthep is the International Buddhist Center, which runs meditation and study courses throughout the year.

Open Daily
Entrance: 30 Baht

DOI PUI

The whole mountain area that Wat Doi Suthep sits within is called the Doi Suthep-Pui National Park. At 1,685 meters above sea level, Doi Pui is the highest peak in the park and is home to a stunning landscape, wildlife and waterfalls. Most waterfalls are well signed for tourists making their own way up the mountain and going past Wat Doi Suthep leads you to the Phuping Palace, and to the interesting Hmong tribal village. The village offers a chance to see Hmong natives in their traditional dress, try their local dishes and purchase some handicrafts made in local villages.

PHUPING PALACE

Phuping Palace is the Winter Residence of the Thai Royal Family. Temperatures up the mountain are cooler, so winter feels cool and fresh, and in the summer it is a pleasant respite from the hot city air. Parts of the palace are open to the public as well, including the well manicured gardens, which feature rare Asian flowers.

Open daily 8:30 - 16:30 (usually closed January to March)
Entrance: 50 Baht

CHEDI LUANG

If you're short on time or have already visited Wat Doi Suthep and need more temple action, then head to Wat Chedi Luang – one of the most interesting temples located right in the middle of the Old City. 'Luang' translates in old Lanna language meaning 'very large', and the enormous crumbling structure translates correctly. The main Chedi is 80 metres and the highest point in Chiang Mai's old city. The original temple dates back to 1385 but what you see today has had many additions and alterations, as well as rebuilds after invasions. An earthquake in the 1500s brought almost half the temple down, but it was rebuilt over the years to its original size, finishing the renovation as late as 1992. However, the original Chedi is still not in perfect condition and serves as a reminder that all things eventually age. The temple used to house the Emerald Buddha at the top of the crumbling Chedi, but now sits in Bangkok's Grand Palace.

Open: 6:00 - 17:00
Location: Phrapokklao Road

WAT PHRA SINGH

Wat Phra Singh is perhaps the second most sacred temple in Chiang Mai after Wat Doi Suthep. It houses three main structures, the main attraction being the elegantly decorated Lai Kam assembly hall and its restored murals depicting the lives of locals hundreds of years ago. Located inside the old city wall, at the western end of Ratchadamnoen Road (also known as the Sunday Walking Street), the temple's signature Lanna-style roofs and glittering assembly hall invite visitors into the temple grounds. The larger main assembly hall houses a 15th-Century Buddha image cast from copper and gold.

Open: 06:00-17:00
Location: Inside the Old City, Ratchadamnoen Road

THAPAE GATE & THE FORTRESS WALL

Thapae Gate is one of the most famous landmarks in Chiang Mai and is part of the crumbling city wall, which once acted as a fortress for the 'Old City' (and today still acts as a geographical boundary). The gate area is a tourist epicentre in Chiang Mai, boasting more hotels, bars, restaurants, cafes, massage parlours and shops than anywhere else in the city, including the first Starbucks in Northern Thailand. It's best to visit Thapae Gate in the early evening as the temperature cools and locals start using it as a public square to hang out in. On Sundays, it is overrun by the Sunday Walking Street, which starts at the Gate and finishes on the other end of the city at Wat Phra Singh. The fortress wall runs along all four sides of the old city of Chiang Mai, and it's hard to miss as main roads run parallel to the moat and the walls are lit up at night time.

Location: Moon Muang Road and Thapae Road

SILVER TEMPLE

The Silver temple, also known as Wat Sri Suphan is an impressive hand crafted silver temple. From the walls to the roof (and everything within the temple), everything has been covered in silver panels – and ornately crafted. While this temple needs to be seen to be believed, the temple is part of a silversmith village that has been operating for over 500 years. While the temple was initially built for the surrounding community and only patched with leftovers from the workshops, in 2008 the process of completely covering it with silver began. Around the silver temple there are lots of small silver studios and real artists at work. In these studios you can buy or commission works of silver to take home. A visit to the Silver temple can be combined with a visit to the Saturday Walking Street.

Open: 6:00 -21:00
Location: 100 Wulai Road

WAT UMONG

An old, crumbling temple complex tucked deep in the woods and a fascinating place to walk around, Wat Umong is one of Chiang Mai's truly hidden gems. Over 700 years old and still a fully functioning monastery, the temple is set among trees, gardens and a large pond. The central stupa is weather worn and looks its age, while the feature piece of the temple, the ancient underground meditation tunnels, are still in excellent condition.

There are always monks walking around, often circling the stupa in prayer. The tunnels are rarely used for meditation anymore due to the amount of visitors that come each day. There are a few enclaves with Buddha statues and if you look on the ceiling of the tunnels you may be able to see some old drawings of elephants and temples, thought to date back to the 13th or 14th Century. To the left of the tunnels is a large lake and a small island that is connected by a bridge. The lake is full of large catfish and by feeding them you gain good merit. There are also a few turtles and it is considered lucky if you spot one of them. While the food is meant for the fish, most people end up feeding the pigeons that live on the island as well.

Open: 06:00 - 17:00
Location: 135 Suthep road, Soi Umong, Suthep

LANNA FOLKLIFE MUSEUM

Close to the Three Kings monument in the centre of Chiang Mai's old city, the Lanna Folklife Museum hosts a permanent exhibition about the people who live and have lived in the Lanna region, exploring daily scenes of life through waxworks and ancient relics. The Lanna Folk Museum is set in a beautiful old courthouse building with a small garden surrounding it. The museum only has two floors and a visit will take around an hour or so. If you plan to visit the Chiang Mai Historical Centre, there's a combo ticket that includes the three city centre museums.

Open: Tue-Sun, 08:30 - 17:00
Location: Phrapokklao Road

CHIANG MAI HISTORICAL CENTRE

Opposite the Lanna Folk Life Museum and just behind the Three Kings Monument is the Chiang Mai Historical Centre. A new museum to Chiang Mai, the exhibitions are well presented and follow the history of the city, including the Lanna Kingdom over the past 700 years.

Opened in 2013, this new museum follows the history of the Lanna, as well as touching on the period before this. This museum has a much more modern feel when compared to the Chiang Mai National Museum, and it presents information in bite-size pieces, which is great for children. The displays come with a spoken introduction in a variety of languages, including English, German, French and Chinese. One of the coolest things about the Chiang Mai Historical Centre is that when it was being built the workers discovered an old royal temple underneath. They decided to preserve it and the addition helps to bring a little slice of history to life.

Open: Tue-Sun, 08:30 - 17:00
Location: Ratvithi Road, next to the Arts and Culture Museum and former City Hall

CHIANG MAI UNIVERSITY

Chiang Mai University is a beautiful, green campus at the foot of the mountain and one of the most popular places to visit for Chinese tourists. The campus supplies regular tours on electric buses for tourists, and it's the best way to view the University. The main entrance to the university is on Huey Kaew Road. This is the only entrance that tourists can enter, and it's also the starting point of the tour. The main gate is often decorated with colourful flowers and the university sign written in Thai is a popular place to pose for pictures. Parking inside the university costs 100 Baht for motorbikes for 4 hours costs and 200 Baht for cars. The electric buses run tours of Chiang Mai University every half hour (or more during busy times). The tour costs 50 Baht for adults and 20 Baht for children. The tour takes around 40 minutes and offers a detailed description of buildings, departments, and the history of the university while customers can take pictures and see the beauty of the University. There is one stop allowing customers to get off the bus and take pictures at Angkaew Reservoir, a large artificial lake with a backdrop of Doi Pui mountain. It might sound strange that a university is a tourist attraction, but with large gardens, a reservoir and some listed buildings there is plenty to see inside the grounds of CMU.

Open: 9:00 – 17:00
Location: Chiang Mai University 239, Huay Kaew Road

WIANG KUM KAM

One of Chiang Mai's hidden gems, Wat Kum Kam sits peacefully along the the Ping River about 5 km south of Chiang Mai city. Wiang Kum Kam is an ancient city dating back to the 8th century, and served as the unofficial capital of the Lanna Kingdom until Chiang Mai was officially chosen in 1296. The centrepiece of the area is Wat Chedi Liam, and highlights early Lanna style. The pavilion takes on a Burmese style thanks to the traders who restored it in the 1900s. Some of the stone tablets are engraved with Mon or Sanskrit writing and the spirit house of King Mengrai (the founder of Chiang Mai) is located in Wat Chang Kham. The most popular way to see Wiang Kum Kam is by horse-drawn carriage tour, although bicycles are also available for hire.

Open: 08:00 – 17:00
Location: About five km southeast of the Old City (take Route 106, or Chiang Mai – Lamphun Highway, from Chiang Mai City)

ART IN PARADISE

The Art in Paradise Museum Chiang Mai is one of the most fun places in the city to take photographs with your partner or friends. The museum has over 130 different images of illusions – paintings drawn to create a 3D image which allows people to seem as if they are really in the picture. It is one of the biggest 3D museums in the world, spanning three floors. There are six different zones in the museum including the underwater world, wildlife area, classic art, ancient Egypt, surreal art, and the dinosaur zone. Visitors can take a range of unique photos that have been creatively designed and painted onto the walls and floors of the museum. It takes a minimum of two hours to visit all the zones but many people spend more time there. The exterior itself is a large stone building, which looks out of place compared to the Thai buildings around it. The inside is air conditioned and there is a restaurant and a coffee shop available before or after museum visits.

Cost: 300 Baht (adults)
Open: 09.00 – 21.00
Location: 199/9 Chang Klan Road, Chang Klan

CHIANG MAI NIGHT SAFARI

Modeled after the successful Singapore Night Safari, the Chiang Mai Night Safari park is equally thrilling and houses some amazing animals native to Thailand. There are three different animal zones – Savanna Safari, Predator Prowl and Jaguar Trail – that visitors tour around in an open sided tram. The Predator Prowl cuts right into the heart of the wilderness and lets you meet some fierce predators from Bengali tigers, pumas and lions, to hyenas, bears, wild boars and deer. You can also walk parts of the tour, which make you really feel as if you are in the middle of the jungle at night. There are many other milder activities, such as petting tiger cubs, a laser light show, as well as a great restaurant on the grounds.

Open: 11.00 – 23.00
Location: Hangdong, southwest of Chiang Mai International Airport

QUEEN SIRIKIT BOTANICAL GARDEN

The Queen Sirikit Botanical Garden, located 30 minutes north of Chiang Mai, is a centre to promote research, biodiversity and allows visitors to see the most diverse natural plants that Thailand has to offer. The garden is set in a valley surrounded by rainforest and there is a whole range of different areas to visit. Visitors can walk around the flower gardens, banana path or enter one of the many different greenhouses – Savanna House, Orchid House or the Carnivorous Plant House. Another highlight of the gardens is a 400 metre canopy walkway, which is suspended over the jungle canopy and gives an enlightening perspective of nature from high up in the air.

If you don't feel like walking around the area, there is the option to take your motorbike (30 Baht) or car (50 Baht) into Queen Sirikit Botanical Garden. The gardens are huge and you will need transportation if you want to see it all in one day. If you don't have your own car, a shuttle bus is available and has stops at each section. You should plan at least 3 hours to visit Queen Sirikit Botanical Gardens but you could spend the whole day here because there is so much to see.

Open: 8:30 - 16:30
Location: 100 moo 9, Highway 1096, Mae Rim

CHIANG MAI ZOO

A small but enjoyable afternoon trip, Chiang Mai zoo has been a staple on the tourist trail for the last 40 odd years. Located at the foot of Doi Pui mountain, the elephants, zebras, hippos, giraffes, rhinos and deer all enjoy mountain views and cooler temperatures from their spacious pens. A large zoo by size, with an aquarium, aviary, panda house (with pandas on loan from China) and a snow dome, more popular with Thai's than tourists. There used to be a monorail, but it is currently out of order due to the owner wanting more money to run the rail, so guests can walk or take the electric bus around the zoo, which takes around 2 hours to navigate.

Open: 8:00 - 17:00
Location: Huey Kaew Road, next to Chiang Mai University

ACTIVITIES

While Chiang Mai has lots to see in the city, there is even more adventure to be had in its surroundings. From nature treks in the jungle, cascading waterfalls and elephant herds, to ziplining, climbing, caving and even white water rafting - there are countless activities to meet your adventure levels. The following activities are only a glimpse into what is possible, and most activities can be booked online or through your hotel and will arrange transportation and food. All you need to do is decide on which activity you want to experience.

LUXURIOUS CHIANG MAI

FLIGHT OF THE GIBBON ZIPLINE

One of the most fun and unique activities in Chiang Mai, ziplining lets you explore the rainforests of Northern Thailand from within the canopy. Flight of the Gibbon was the first to offer zipline tours in the jungles as a way to raise money and create a sanctuary for gibbons in the region. Today, it is one of the best ziplines in the world and despite many imitations, Flight of the Gibbon remains the best.

The tour involves ziplining between treetop platforms and rappelling descents. Guests can combine the zipline with other activities such as river rafting, mountain biking and rock climbing (or just organise them separately). Flight of the Gibbon focuses on being educational as well as fun – visitors learn about the local animals on the animal safari tour. With locations in Chiang Mai, Bangkok, and Pattaya, you can zip your way through the country. Maybe the best part is that the money you pay to experience the jungles of Thailand goes towards protecting them — 10% of Flight of the Gibbon's profits go to protecting the endangered gibbon and the rain forest it calls home. Tours start at 3,999 Baht per person.

www.treetopasia.com/thailand-holiday/chiang-mai

ELEPHANT RIDING

Elephants are the national symbol of Thailand and no trip to the north would be complete without meeting one of these gentle giants up close. Most elephants in Thailand reside in the north where there is more space and food for them, although there are few in southern national parks. The biggest issue when riding or meeting elephants is whether the camp is authentic and caring towards the elephants or just out for profit. While riding on a chair can hurt an elephant, bareback is usually okay for them. However a no harm but super fun activity is bathing with elephants – it's a fun chance to actually play with the elephants, splash them and watch them dive into rivers and streams. Of course they will also splash and spray you in return for your efforts.

THAI ELEPHANT CONSERVATION CENTER (TECC)

Located about 40 minutes from Chiang Mai, the Thai Elephant Conservation Center (TECC) in Lampang is the only Government owned elephant centre in Thailand. This means that on most days it is packed with school children, enjoying the beauty of elephants like we all should. Most of the residents at TECC are orphans or rescued from other camps in the region. In the mornings the elephants are bathed and visitors can ride and bathe with them if they wish. After that the elephants walk over to an arena and perform a show for visitors. From painting pictures, balancing on logs to bowing to the crowd, the elephants are kept stimulated and seem to enjoy the act of performing, with their skills shown off to the audience. The impressive paintings by the elephants can be purchased from the shop (with profits going back into caring for the elephants). The morning at TECC starts early and the elephants return to the jungle around 3pm for an afternoon of relaxation without people.

www.thailandelephant.org/en/

ELEPHANT NATURE PARK

The Elephant Nature Park is an amazing rehabilitation centre focused on providing a natural environment for elephants, dogs, cats, buffaloes and many other abused animals. As well as single day visits the Park can organise short volunteer programs which allow you to really see the life of an elephant and the reality of their upkeep. This place is recommended for all animal lovers. Located an hour north of Chiang Mai, visiting Elephant Nature Park can be combined with a trip to **Chiang Dao**.

www.elephantnaturepark.org

THE ELEPHANT JUNGLE SANCTUARY

The Elephant Jungle Sanctuary is an ethical and sustainable eco-tourism project located an hour away from Chiang Mai. A relatively new and admirable project started to improve the welfare and conditions of Elephants. They have two locations, one is in Phuket. The Sanctuary is firm on its no riding policy and focuses on creating an environment where elephants can enjoy their lives, while educating tourists and locals about proper elephant care.

www.elephantjunglesanctuary.com/

If you want to experience living in luxury within the jungle while meeting elephants in their natural habitat then consider the Four Seasons Tented Camp or Anantara Elephant camp in Chiang Rai (see trips out of Chiang Mai chapter), with both resorts sharing an elephant camp.

MOTORBIKING

Thailand is full of scooters and motorbikes and those who love to ride will be in awe of the world class winding roads. Good quality motorbikes can be hired all over Chiang Mai, and you can ask your hotel to arrange a drop off of the bike you want to drive. From Chiang Mai city, there are lots of interesting roads to take, from driving up to Doi Suthep or Doi Inthanon, doing the Samoeng loop, a winding mountainous road which circles behind Doi Pui mountain, Chiang Dao or even to to Doi Ang Khang – the top of Thailand. Once you get out of the city, the roads are mostly empty. Check www.gt-rider.com for information or to find a touring group.

MONK CHAT

The Monk Chat programs are a great way to learn about the Buddhist culture in Thailand and ask all those questions about temples and Buddhist life that you've wanted answered. Monk Chat occurs at a few different temples in Chiang Mai, often in the evenings. The most popular chat is at Wat Suan Dok, which also has a Buddhist school and is trying to help novice monks improve their English language skills by speaking with native speakers. Both men and women are welcome to join monk chats and they are donation based. Monk Chat sessions are held every Monday, Wednesday and Friday from 1700 – 1900 at Wat Suan Dok, Suthep Road.

HOT AIR BALLOON

Flying in a hot air balloon is a once in a lifetime experience, especially in a free floating balloon. Flying, or rather gliding over rice paddies and golden temples while admiring the 360 degree view of green, mist covered mountains is a unique experience that should be on the top of every visitor's list when visiting Chiang

Mai. The Balloon Adventure starts in the countryside of Chiang Mai, seeing the city from a distance, and you steadily rise to between 1,000 and 2,000 feet. As you rise into the air and float up through the morning clouds, guests are rewarded with panoramic views of the local countryside, glittering temples and the city from above. A friendly captain, cool morning breeze and a feeling of peace and serenity as you rise above it all are highlights to this magical ride, and it's one of the best ways to experience Chiang Mai and the beauty of northern Thailand. Balloon Adventure Thailand will arrange the transfer from your hotel, and also supply a buffet breakfast and champagne after your successful flight. While the celebration is routine, the captain is a veteran in his field and has flown balloons all over the world. From 6am until around 9am you are taken care of and treated to a glimpse of Thai hospitality, as well as a beautiful view of Thailand from above. A flight in a hot air balloon will add to your memories of Chiang Mai, and many guests arrange a wedding proposal in the air. Balloon Adventure has been arranging proposal flights for hundreds of couples already and handles all aspects from flowers to keeping the proposal a secret. A day in a balloon should be on everyone's Chiang Mai adventure list!

www.balloonadventurethailand.com
Tel: 089 685 1188

YOGA

No trip would be complete without taking a yoga class. Most hotels can arrange private classes for beginners (or couples), but for the seasoned yogi then consider either Wild Rose or even booking onto a yoga retreat as part of your holiday.

WILD ROSE STUDIO

For any experienced yogi Wild Rose Studio is a dream. A combination of excellent teachers in a unique traditional wooden Thai house in the heart of the old city, taking a class here is unforgettable. One of the firm favourites for yogi's travelling to Chiang Mai, Wild Rose offers mid morning and evening classes most days of the week. While the single studio room is limited to around 16 people, each person always receives personal attention from either Rose or her staff members. The studio has a small changing room and showers as well as counter selling beautiful handmade jewellery and information about local businesses. Check the website for the latest schedule and then prepare to be stretched and strengthened.

www.wildroseyoga.org/calendar

THAILAND YOGA HOLIDAYS

If you love yoga and are falling in love with Thailand during your trip then why not consider taking a yoga inspired holiday. An exclusive chance to discover Northern Thailand while deepening your practice Thailand Yoga Holidays offers some of the most luxurious retreats available. A combination of yoga, relaxation, culture and healthy food participants get a chance to explore both their spiritual side and the nature of Thailand. Regular retreats are run throughout the year and there is also the option of designing your own dream retreat. See the Thailand Yoga Holidays website for more information and quote *LuxuriousChiangMaiBook* for a 5,000 Baht discount.

www.thailandyogaholidays.com

COOKING SCHOOLS

Taking a cooking course is a must for anyone visiting Chiang Mai, as it is said this is the best city in south east Asia for food! From the Northern Khao Soi delight, to all kinds of rich curries, Chiang Mai offers a range of dishes not found elsewhere in Thailand. Many luxury hotels have cooking schools within their grounds, so you don't even need to leave the hotel to try your hand at cooking (and then eating) some Thai specialties. The Four Seasons in Mae Rim offers an exquisite 10 course meal at the Chef's Table. The hotels chef talks guest through each dish as well as inviting guests into her kitchen as she demonstrates how to cook each dish right in front of you using the freshest ingredients. This is a memorable experience and a great way to sample Thai cooking and cuisine without having to actually cook. However, if you wish to explore more of Thai cuisine and feel like a change of scenery try one of these great cooking schools.

THE CHIANG MAI THAI COOKERY SCHOOL

The first cooking school in Northern Thailand, The Chiang Mai Thai Cookery School has one of the best reputations in town. Run by one of Thailand's famous chefs, Sompon Nabnian, the school hosts a variety of cooking classes, from beginners and advanced, and also offers a homestay for those who wish to study over a longer period of time. The Chiang Mai Thai Cookery School has been operating for over 13 years and is the place to go for chefs and people serious about cooking. Courses start at 1,450 Baht per person, with advanced courses starting at 3,000 Baht and taught by Sompon himself.

www.thaicookeryschool.com
Tel: +66 (0)532 06388

MAY KAIDEE'S COOKING SCHOOL

May Kaidee's Cooking School is run by a famous Thai chef specialising in vegetarian and vegan dishes. The original cooking school started in Bangkok in 1988 and runs simultaneous courses in Chiang Mai and Bangkok daily. May Kaidee's features two classes a day, including an introduction and small talk about how to make chili paste and the use of Thai herbs and spices. Then, participants learn how to cook different recipes and taste their dishes. After cooking and eating, participants will then get to see a traditional Thai dancing show and are served a complimentary mango and sticky rice dessert. The most popular class, Thai cooking, costs 1,500 Baht per person and quickly sells out during peak season. In Bangkok, there are even more courses including 5-10 day workshops, tofu making and raw food classes as well as pampering travel packages.

www.maykaidee.com/cooking-school
Tel: +66 (0) 53 232 696

GOLF

Chiang Mai isn't known as a golfing haven, but for those who love to play, Chiang Mai is as good a place as any. With Doi Pui mountain as a backdrop, and less competition on the grass, golf enthusiasts can enjoy days of fun in Northern Thailand.

ROYAL CHIANG MAI

Opened back in 1996, Royal Chiang Mai is an ever popular course designed by five-times British Open champion Mr. Peter Thompson. The course is demanding and is better for accurate and skilled golfers. Don't let this put you off though, as the 18 hole course is enjoyable and strategic.

www.royalchiangmai.com

NORTH HILL CITY RESORT

A hotel and Golf resort 30 minutes from Chiang Mai city, North Hill offers beautiful scenery, rolling greens and an interesting 18 hole, par-72 strategic course including sand and streams to overcome. Equipment and caddies can be rented, or you can bring your own clubs.

www.northhillcityresort.com

CHIANG MAI HIGHLANDS

A little east of Chiang Mai is a 27 hole championship golf course, offering a good course and nature views. Designed by Schmidt-Curley Golf Design, Chiang Mai Highlands is among the top 10 courses to play in Thailand.

www.chiangmaihighlands.com/golf/

CHIANGMAI INTHANON GOLF AND NATURAL RESORT

Playing at the foot of Thailand's highest mountain, Chiangmai Inthanon Golf and Natural Resort is a popular spot for Thai golfers and tourists. 18 holes and some challenges, this is a an enjoyable day out and can be combined with a visit to Doi Inthanon.

www.chiangmaiinthanongolfresort.com

CHIANG MAI NATURE

Thailand boasts some stunning scenery (think of the movie 'The Beach', or open any travel magazine), from beaches to rainforest, waterfalls to hidden lakes. Even if you are a city person, you should still try to experience some of Northern Thailand's majestic nature. From Chiang Mai in every direction there are stunning green vistas, rice paddies, rolling mountains and natural wonders. If you are a nature lover then the following places are some beautiful spots to discover.

DOI PUI VIEWPOINTS

Rent a motorbike or a car and spend the day meandering up doi Pui mountain. Stop at the various viewpoints along the way and both the left and right turns at the junctions - there is more to see on the mountain than just Doi Suthep. Thanks to the high elevation, Doi Pui is usually covered in mist and has a cooler climate compared to Chiang Mai (average temperatures of 20 - 23 degrees Celsius but it can get very cold in Dec/Jan). The forest cover consists of mixed deciduous and evergreen forests, with bursts of colourful blossoms dotting the entire mountain slopes. In late January there is a blossoming of Sakura flowers on Doi Pui. Various species of birds and small mammals inhabit the forests, among them red jungle fowl, pheasants, eagles, wild boar and macaque. Driving up the mountain allows you to be in the middle of the dense protected forest and through the trees you can glimpse Chiang Mai from below. A 10 minute drive after the famous Wat Phra That Doi Suthep is the Hmong Tribal Village. A great place to explore local hilltribe life and culture through their musical instruments, costumes and bamboo crafts on offer. Doi Pui's Hmong people used to cultivate opium poppies for a livelihood, but the Royal Project sustainable agriculture projects transformed the entire village to agricultural farms and today the Hmong villagers generate their income from selling agricultural products as well as tribal souvenirs to visitors.

HUEY KAEW WATERFALL

At the base of Doi Pui mountain, at the end of Huey Kaew road and the next to the zoo is Huey Kaew waterfall. The waterfall is free to enter and the closest one to the city. It may not be the most impressive waterfall but it is pretty and if you are lucky and it isn't crowded then it is a good place to spend an afternoon in nature. From the waterfall you can also follow the hiking trail all the way to Wat Doi Suthep.

GRAND CANYON

Chiang Mai's Grand Canyon is about 40 minutes south of the city and one of Chiang Mai's hidden gems. An old limestone quarry, the area has been flooded over the years and is now a popular swimming and diving spot. The canyon is no longer Chiang Mai's best kept secret and there is now an entrance fee that goes towards improving safety in the area. There is also a giant water park next door and the canyon itself has lost all its unique charm. However the area around the grand canyon is interesting and there are smaller quarries around the streets so it is worth the drive out of the city. The best way to get there is by renting a motorbike as there is no public transport to that area. Driving south along Canal Road, look out for signs suggesting a right turn to the canyon after about 20 minutes.

HUEY TUNG TAO

A large artificial lake with views of the rolling mountains, Huey Tung Tao is a nature lover's heaven. Spend all day relaxing in the bamboo huts, eating som tam (papaya salad) and drinking beer, drive or walk around the lake. Huay Tung Tao lake has a two lane road running in circular around the lake which is perfect for cyclists, joggers and walkers. The water in the lake is not very clean but at certain points near the bamboo bungalows you can swim or dip your feet in the water. Because of the scenery many people come to Huay Tung Tao for the day and have lunch at one of the many restaurants. Each restaurant has a few bamboo bungalows and they are free to sit in as long as you order off the menu. There are also vendors who walk around selling fruit, fried insects and ice cream. The lake is open until sunset and just off Canal Road going north to Mae Rim.

BUA TONG WATERFALL

Bua Thong Waterfall is a unique, multi-tiered waterfall made of limestone and mineral deposits. It has been nicknamed 'the sticky waterfall' because the limestone creates friction to stop slipping, making it very easy to climb up the waterfall. The limestone is slightly rough but it isn't painful to step on, and forms an wonderful bubbly pattern. There are 5 different levels to experience and steps on the side of the waterfall leading all the way to the bottom. Most people walk to the bottom and then climb up the waterfall to the top. On a hot and humid day the water is cool and refreshing. While many people wear swimsuits and explore the waterfall, there is lots to do if you don't want to climb up Bua Tong. At the entrance is a picnic spot and a few restaurants, and many Thai people spend the entire day at Bua Thong Waterfall, eating and drinking. There is also a pleasant walk from the picnic area leading to a shrine with a few pools of crystal clean water from the waterfall, butterflies and birds along the way. The waterfall is about an hour from Chiang Mai by car and is located in Mae Tang district on highway 1001.

DOI INTHANON

Standing at 2,565 Metres (8, 415 feet), Doi Inthanon is the highest peak in Thailand, and often recorded as one of the coldest places too. It is common to see Thai's wrapped in ski jackets and winter hats in June, enjoying the brisk air as a change from sweltering temperatures in the summer months. Doi Inthanon National Park is a true jewel of natural beauty, consisting of rugged mountainous terrain covered by lush tropical forests and dotted with rivers and waterfalls. The park's protected status makes it a sanctuary for a wide range of animal species, and it is perhaps the best place in Thailand for bird watching. Approximately 362 different bird species make their home in Doi Inthanon National Park, many of which are not found anywhere else in Thailand.

Modern and elegant Chedis are perched on the peak of the mountain, dedicated to the Royal King and Queen and the inside of the Chedis have been adapted into exhibition halls. There are some restaurants and beautiful gardens to stroll around in, but most of the natural beauty of the environment has been preserved.

PHRA CHOR CANYON

A secret spot, still mostly undiscovered by tourists, Phra Chor Canyon is a naturally occurring canyon wall that resembles pillars carved into rock. Part of the Mae Wang National Park, a 10 minute drive from the main road and a 15 minute walk will get you to the highlight of the canyon. The sandstone cliffs are between 30 and 40 metres high, and the walkway takes you right to the bottom of the canyon, offering an impressive scale to see the cliffs at. There is a small loop to walk through the empty riverbed that once carved these rocks, and parts of the walk lead through tight spots and over rocks. To drive there, take highway 108 south and then turn right on highway 12039 to Mae Wang National Park. It's a good idea to combine visiting Phra Chor with a trip to Doi Inthanon, and most hotels can arrange a driver for the day.

MAE SA VALLEY

Mae Sa Valley is a green, forested area north of Doi Pui mountain. There is a windy road running through the valley and lots of tourist activities scattered along the road. The highway 1096 runs from Mae Rim (about 10KM from Chiang Mai) to the town of Samoeng which is a popular destination for motorbike day trippers traveling the Sameong Loop. Many people stop along the way at attractions in Mae Sa Valley including the X-Centre offering action packed activities like bungee jumping, zip lining, driving ATV's, zorbing and paint balling. There are also lots of nature orientated activities in the Mae Sa Valley such as visiting elephant camps, the Queen Sirikit Botanical Garden, Elephant Poo Poo Paper Park and the popular eight-tiered Mae Sa Waterfall. If you like animals then Mae Sa Valley has the Tiger Kingdom (where you can pose for a picture with a tiger), the Mae Rim Monkey School, Mae Sa Snake Farm and the Orchid & Butterfly Farm.

MAE SA WATERFALL

Mae Sa Waterfall is an impressive eight tiered waterfall nestled deep in the jungle. The entrance costs 200 Baht for foreigners but it's a big waterfall with a plunge pool for swimming, and you can pack a blanket or picnic and spend a day at the waterfall. There is a large parking lot with lots of street vendors selling grilled pork and sticky rice, fruit, bottled drinks and ice cream. Popular with both Thai's and tourists the waterfall can get busy on weekends with families. If you climb up to the fifth or sixth level there are less people and at the top of the waterfall there are hardly any people so it's a nice place to get away from the crowds. Mae Sa Waterfall is located about 30 minutes away from Chiang Mai by car on the Mae Rim - Samoeng Road. While the waterfall is not visible from the road, there are lots of signs that point the way.

MON CHAM

Mon Cham is a mountaintop viewpoint and restaurant that has beautiful views over the Mae Rim Valley and Royal Project farms. An hour's drive away from Chiang Mai, Mon Cham and can be reached by car or motorbike. The road going up to the viewpoint is quite steep so it is not recommended for new drivers. Mon Cham is sometimes written as Mon Jam or Mon Jaem, which can be confusing when trying to get there. The top of Mon Cham has a restaurant, a parking area and lots of scenic places to sit, admire the 360 degree view or take photos. There are lots of flowers being grown there so its is very colourful. The restaurant serves mostly Thai food and some interesting salads with edible flowers, and there are bamboo huts with great views to sit and eat in. The menu changes regularly and is written on a white board in Thai. There is some English translation and there is also a basic English menu available. Mon Cham is open from 10:00 until sunset and to get there turn off highway 1096 and follow signs to Mon Cham Royal Project.

ROYAL FLORA RATCHAPHRUEK

A large park a little south of Chiang Mai, Royal Flora Ratchaphruek is heaven for those who enjoy seeing rare varieties of flowers from Asia. Royal Flora Ratchaphruek hosts Southeast Asia's biggest horticultural exposition yearly and so the park is always ready to show its colours to visitors, no matter the season. Over 80 hectares of gardens display varieties of flowers, trees and regional plants, and the park itself is named after one of Thailand's national flower; Cassia fistula, the golden shower tree. The park encloses a few botanical gardens, each with a different theme, has ponds with lotus flowers, orchid pavilions and at the centre of the park stands the impressive teak Ho Kham Royal Pavilion. It can get hot at Royal Flora Ratchaphruek so be sure to bring a hat or an umbrella as there aren't many shaded areas. Visitors can rent bicycles or use the electric bus that makes a regular route around the park. Royal Flora Ratchaphruek is open daily from 9:00 to 20:00 and is close to the Night Safari in Mae Hia district.

ART GALLERIES

Art can be found all over Chiang Mai, but it is usually for sale or as part of a cafe. Both Tita Gallery and Woo Cafe (see cafes and high tea section) offer exhibition spaces to visit in conjunction with their cafe. The following places are the best options to find art in Chiang Mai, but it is wise to call ahead as 'official' opening hours don't mean much to artists living on Thai time.

THAPAE EAST

A unique venue holding a variety of different shows, concerts, events and gatherings - Thapae East is where Chiang Mai's artists hang out. A space with an orange metal shell, Thapae East is open to the elements, but a flexible space to create a different feel each time, from hay barrels to fairy lights, jazz to DJ's, each event feels different and Thapae East truly is a 'venue for the creative arts'.

Open: daily
Location: 88 Thapae Road, Soi 3
Tel: 091-853-4101
Website: www.facebook.com/ThapaeEast

SUVANNABHUMI ART GALLERY

Over the river from the old city stands to the unobtrusive Suvannabhumi Art Gallery, filled with cultural art from Burma. An unusual shop in the northern Lanna kingdom, the art here is unique and expressive in ways that artists within Myanmar are unable to create. A great space to enter into a different culture.

Open: 10:00 - 19:00
Location: 116 Chareonrat Road, Watgate
Tel: +66 (0) 810 315 309
Website: www.suvannabhumiartgallery.com

MEETING ROOM CAFE

The meeting room is a wonderful space for art and book lovers. One wall is comprised of bookshelf with Thai, English, French and other language books, while the rest of the space is full of art pieces, paintings and fine wines. The space is primarily a shop but there are a few spaces to sit and drink coffee while pondering the artwork. The traditional building is also impressive and there is a small space which holds local exhibitions.

Open: 9:00 -20:00
Location: 89 Charoen Raj Road, Wat Gate
Tel: (+66) 080 627 9219

GALERIE PANISA

Founded in 2002 by the Chindasilpa family members from their love of art and northern Thailand, this gallery has around 6 exhibitions yearly from renowned Thai and foreign artists. The gallery itself sits in a sleek Lanna style house with a large green garden. It's wise to make an appointment before visiting.

Open: 9:00 - 18:00 (closed Sundays)
Location: 189 Mahidol Road, Haiya
Tel:+66 (0) 53 202 779
Website: www.panisa.net

MAIIAM

Chiang Mai's contemporary art museum opened in 2016 and has already had some wonderful and controversial exhibitions pass through its doors. A 20-minute drive from Chiang Mai, Maiiam is located in a warehouse like building and hopes to become one of the top museums in Thailand, already lining up some famous Thai artists. The owner of Maiiam is also the marketing director of the Jim Thompson brand, and so everything is in both English and Thai.

Open: 10:00 - 18:00 (closed Tuesdays)
Location: 22 Moo 7 Tonpao, Sankampheang
Website: www.maiiam.com

GALLERY SEESCAPE

A long standing Nimman art gallery, this space stands alone in the increasingly modernising Nimmanhaemin area. Part cafe, part shop and part art gallery, there is lots to see in this corner of soi 17. New shows open roughly once every quarter so check their facebook page for what's happening.

Open: Daily
Location: 22/1 Nimmanhemin Road, Soi 17
Tel: 093-831-9394
Website: www.facebook.com/galleryseescape

WATTANA ART GALLERY

A cool and highly regarded art studio, Wattana's art gallery is hidden in the leafy area near to Chiang Mai University. With an online shop, most of his art can be bought and shipped abroad but if you get the chance, a visit to the studio is well worth it. While there are opening hours, it's best to phone ahead for an official appointment.

Open: 8:30 - 16:30
Location: 100/1 Moo10, Soi Wat Umong, Suthep Road
Tel: 089 429 1883
Website: www.wattana-art.com

FINE DINING

Many of the five star hotels in Thailand also do fine dining extremely well. As a country that excels in hospitality and a cuisine rated as one of the best in the world, eating in Thailand is considered a national pastime and eating well has become a popular luxury for everyone. Thai cuisine is varied in tastes, flavours and options, with spring rolls for snacks, mango and sticky rice for dessert and a colourful range of spicy, sweet or sour curries for the main meal. Then there are hundreds of different noodle dishes, as well as salads, dips, roasted meats and stir fries. Food is available at all times of the day and night, and a trip to Thailand would not be complete without a meal at a street cart. However Chiang Mai also has some amazing restaurants at a fraction of western prices, and these cuisines include Italian, French, European and even Chinese. So while good food can be found at almost every restaurant in Chiang Mai, luxurious fine dining is worth splurging on, especially for visitors who love fine dining and consider themselves 'foodies'.

ITALICS

An elegant setting and great location (especially for guests of Akyra Manor hotel upstairs) Italics is one of the best restaurants in the Nimmanhaemin area. A large, innovative menu offering both Italian and Thai specialities is to be expected at Italics restaurant. What is surprising are the size of the candlestick decorations, the quality of the locally sourced ingredients and the extensive and varied delicacies served up by chef Phubase and his expert team. The menu has been designed to look like a magazine, and while the first page advertises their excellent breakfast, the second page offers a selection of aperitivo including a cold cuts platter featuring imported ham and Chiang Rai cheese. The salads are distinctly mediterranean, in taste and colours, with vibrant ingredients sourced from Thailand to offer the freshest ingredients possible. A must try are their artisan appetisers, which blend western and Asian delights to perfection. The main meals consist of pasta dishes, pizza and a range of thai food (including the northern delight Khao Soi). For those who love coffee a must try is the coffee braised short rib pork with crispy home made gnocchi. Meals come served on stylish granite plates, which perfectly fit the ultra-modern vibe of the restaurant. As to be expected, their dessert is as good as their main menu, with exotic selections such as mango panna cotta and banana ricotta cheesecake. And then there is the rather substantial drinks list with cocktails that could double as dessert. The atmosphere and food at Italics is already impressive but if you want to really treat yourself then Akyra Manor can organise a private dining experience for up to 12 people at the Chef's table with

Chef Phubase himself. A stunning, customised menu will be designed based on personal tastes along with a suitable wine pairing for dishes. Perfect for special occasions.

www.theakyra.com/chiang-mai/dining/akyra-manor-italics/
Open: 11:00 - 23:00
Location: 22/2 Nimmanhaemin Road Soi 9
Tel: +66 (0) 2 514 8112

DAVID'S KITCHEN

David's Kitchen is rated as one of the finest restaurants in Chiang Mai, and definitely the most popular, winning Thailand's best restaurant (voted by TripAdvisor) for three years in a row and one of Asia's 10 best restaurants.

The head chef at DK David's Kitchen formerly worked at the Mandarin Oriental hotel in Chiang Mai prior to partnering with David to create the original restaurant. The location of the restaurant has moved since its beginning, and the service keeps getting better.

The menu is a mix of French, European, Thai and fusion food, with a separate wine menu . There is also a daily set three course menu, which changes regularly. Every dish is delightful at David's Kitchen, but it is the atmosphere of the restaurant, attention to detail, and the excellent service that makes David's Kitchen one of the best restaurants in the city. If the owner David is present, he greets all his guests personally at their table. Try the risotto with wild mushrooms and white truffle foam, or the grilled duck breast with mashed potato. If you are considering visiting David's Kitchen it's a good idea to book a table in advance as it's always popular and busy. The staff print off your names and add a greeting to your reserved table. It's the perfect honeymoon surprise.

www.davidskitchen.co.th
Open: Monday – Saturday 17:00 – 22:00
Location: 113 Bamrungrad Road, Wat Gate
Tel: +66 (0) 910681744

GINGER & KAFE AT THE HOUSE

A confusing but wonderful combination of clothing, homewares, café and restaurant, The House complex is central but surprisingly overlooked by many visitors to Chiang Mai. While Ginger (see the shopping section) offers some colourful clothing, the adjoining café and restaurant serve some excellent dishes in an elegant setting. The House is a converted building with part of the rooms serving as shopping areas and the main room and outdoor patio being a quirky café. The shop has an artsy feel, with bright sofas, printed pillows and a warm, homely feel. The House restaurant is in a separate building and serves interesting Asian fusion dishes and western comforts along with some strong and bright cocktails. The interior decoration at The House is also not to be missed with a funky, modern twist to the place and a cool elephant mural stenciled onto the wall.

www.thehousethailand.com/about-ginger-kafe
Open: 11:00 – 23:00
Location: 199 Moonmuang Road
Tel: 053-419-011

TIME AT NA NIRAND

Overlooking the riverside and shaded by Na Nirand Romantic Resort's impressive grandfather tree, Time restaurant is a great place to indulge in good food and relax with good company. Time has both indoor and outdoor seating, as well as a rooftop which offers great views of the Ping river and the resort grounds. Indoors, the restaurant has been styled in industrial chic, with comfortable tables and flowers to offset the industrial vibe. Outside the tables are separated by lavender flowers, and some of the seats face the riverside - a good place to watch the boats go by and let your troubles float away. The upstairs area is a little hot during the daytime but a wonderful place for a sunset cocktail, a romantic dinner or for a night cap as the restaurant is open until midnight.

The menu at Time features a range of Thai and fusion dishes, with each meal made with the finest ingredients. The tom yum soup with prawns is worth a mention for its rich, warm taste, as well as the pomelo salad, and pad thai wrapped in an omelet. The chef also has an interesting take on hunglay curry, adding fresh vegetables and crispy pork to the traditional dish. As well as Thai food there is a range of western on offer including fish and chips and caesar salad. There is even the option to have high tea in the afternoon here, with a mix of sweet and savory options and fine teas to complement the tower of delicious bites. A visit to Time at anytime of the day will leave you feeling satisfied and never wanting to leave the resort.

http://www.nanirand.com/EN/Dining
Open: 11:00 – 00:00
Location :1/1 Soi 9, Charoenprathet Road, Chang Klan
Tel: +66 (0)53 280 988

FARANG SES

Excellent food in stunning surroundings are to be expected from one of the most spectacular hotels in Chiang Mai, Farang Ses at the Dhara Dhevi is as luxurious as you can get. A fine French cuisine designed by Chef Carlos Manuel Gaudencio and his team at at Lycee Hotelier de La Rochelle, the menu serves up some impressive delights, from lobster with radish petals and apple marshmallow to quail stuffed with veal and a side of vegetables and truffles. All the ingredients are sourced for quality and include a range of local and imported options to ensure that menu is one of the most innovative in town. The food is not the only thing at Farang Ses that is spectacular. The restaurant itself is set in a sophisticated glass house lined with teak finishing. The high ceiling is decorated with chandeliers, and smart leather seats add to the overall ambience of the restaurant. Finally pair your meal with an award winning wine and a delectable dessert to ensure a well-rounded and satisfying meal.

www.dharadhevi.com/EN/Dining/4
Open: 18:00 - 22:30 (closed Sundays)
Location: 51/4 Moo 1, Chiang Mai-Sankampaeng Road
Tel: +66 (0) 53 888 888

THE RESTAURANT AT RACHAMANKHA

An elegant and memorable dining experience, The Restaurant is part of Ratchamanka, a secret five star hotel located inside the old city. The Ratchamanka is an impressive setting for lunch or dinner and the courtyard creates a peaceful atmosphere away from the city buzz. The Restaurant offers a menu combining Lanna, Burmese, Shan and Western options and they are served in vintage blue pottery. Like the settings, the menu is simple and dignified with high quality ingredients, good for those who are not interested in fusion or elaborate decorations on their food, rather just good quality dining.

www.rachamankha.com/?page=about_rachamankha_dining
Open: 18:00 - 22:30 (closed Sundays)
Location: 6 Rachamanka Road, Phra Singh
Tel: +66 (0) 53 904 111

PALETTE AT 137 PILLARS HOUSE

The Palette and its sister restaurant, The Dining Room, offer a selection of Thai and western delights in a luxurious setting. The Palette is one refurbished room of the historical East Borneo Company's office, while The Dining Room is a lavish glass walled room set behind the 137 Pillars House. The Palette restaurant can seat up to 20 diners and is an intimate setting perfect for a romantic meal. The menu reflects the name with a variety of bright dishes from pasta to expertly roasted meats and seafood. The Dining Room menu (which can also be ordered from in Palette) consists of more traditional Thai dishes, Asian salads and seasonally adjusted dishes to showcase the best of local harvests.

www.snhcollection.com/137pillarshouse/dining/
Open: 12:00 - 23:00
Location: 2 Soi 1, Nawatgate Road, Wat Gate
Tel: +66 (0) 53 247788

CHINA KITCHEN

Serving up some hot treats, China Kitchen at the Shangri-La hotel has a menu of Szechuan and cantonese dishes to satisfy even Chinese diners. The restaurant is decorated in bright red colours and dark wood, to match the cuisine of bold flavours and spicy dishes, and created a fun, casual and yet modern environment. Currently the only Chinese Szechuan restaurant in Chiang Mai, it is often filled with Chinese diners who love their cuisine enough to search for it abroad. The restaurant has two private rooms and a chef's table with a direct view of the kitchen, ideal for cooking enthusiasts.

If you enjoy hot and spicy food then this the ideal restaurant to test your limits in style, but there is lots on offer for those who don't like spice or pepper, including a full dim sum menu, roasted duck and lots of vegetable dishes. The Chinese chef, Chen Jiang Ming, has over 15 years of experience in the culinary arts and was given an award from China's Vice Prime Minister of the State Council. He can cater for individual tastes to ensure each customer has a unique experience at China Kitchen. There is even a unique range of deserts to soothe a spicy dinner, including rice noodle rolls with mango or steamed pomelo with honey.

www.shangri-la.com/chiangmai/shangrila/dining/restaurants/shang-garden/
Open: 11:30 -14:30 and 18:00 - 22:00
Location: 89/8 Chang Klan Road
Tel: (+66) 053 253 888

NORDEN

A relatively unheard of restaurant located far from the old city, along the superhighway, Norden serves up some spectacular Scandinavian dishes as well as international options too. A sleek, simple and dark interior with wooden tables, the restaurant looks exactly as one would expect from a Nordic restaurant. The chef has worked with some of the best chefs in Scandinavia, and has even cooked for the Swedish Royal family in the past. The menu is a great chance to sample Scandinavian food, with Swedish meatballs being the favourite dish on the menu. There are also more known items such as pizza salads for picky eaters. For those wanting to try new dishes or cuisine, this is a great change from traditional Thai and western food.

www.facebook.com/nordenrestaurantchiangmai
Open: 11:30 -21:00
Location: 39 Superhighway (after the PTT petrol station)

ALLEGRO AND FUJIAN

One of the Dhara Dhevi's many restaurant offerings, Allegro is a regional Italian trattoria serving up homely food to be shared. The dishes range from pizzas and pastas to tuna tartare with avocado, Black Angus beef carpaccio and imported mussels sautéed in white wine. Like traditional Thai food, dishes at Allegro are best enjoyed shared with friends or family, so the more guests at your table the better. Allegro also has a menu of fine wines imported and staff can help you pair your wine to your meal. There are also freshly made Italian desserts to indulge in, choose from tiramisu, panna cotta and torta della nonna. Don't forget to the after dinner espresso.

As well as Allegro, Le Grand Lanna and Farang Ses (see their individual descriptions) the Dhara Dhevi also has Akaligo (meaning timeless in sanskrit) and Fujian, a Contemporary Cantonese and Chinese restaurant on site. Akaligo is a bright open and airy restaurant serving buffet breakfasts and an elaborate Sunday brunch fit for a king. The brunch only happens once a month, on the last sunday of the month between 12:00-15:00. If you are here for the brunch add it to your calendar, it's worth it.

Popular with Chinese tourists, Fujian has been decorated in 19th century Portuguese style and is a delight for those who enjoy elaborate meals. Dim sum is the main meal at Fujian, with bamboo steamers stacked up on each table. As well as dim sum, the menu has all the favourites from the Chinese cuisine, from Hong Kong wonton soup to Peking's famous duck. They even (controversially) have shark fin soup, as well as other live seafood. The restaurant also has private dining rooms that can hold up to 50 guests. Visiting Fujian is like visiting China itself.

http://www.dharadhevi.com/EN/Dining/10

LE COQ D'OR RESTAURANT

Le Coq d'Or restaurant is located at the former estate of William Alfred Wood, the first Honorary British consul in Chiang Mai. Serving up amazing food since 1973, Le Coq d'Or has won countless awards for its fine French cuisine and sophisticated ambience. The restaurant is set in a typical English country house with a large garden area (perfect for weddings and social gatherings), and a choice of two dining rooms with floor to ceiling glass windows for garden views or the cozy and intimate fireplace room. Le Coq d'Or claims to have served every member of the Thai Royal Family over the years which shows that this restaurant is indeed fit for a King. Le Coq d'Or also offers an extensive wine list to sample, and signature dishes to try include the succulent rack of Australian Lamb and the Fin de Claire Oysters.

www.lecoqdorrestaurant.com/en/
Open: 11:00-14:00 and 18:00 - 22:00
Location: 11 Soi 2 Koh Klang Road
Tel: +66 (0) 53 141 555

LE CRYSTAL

One of the longest standing fine dining restaurants in Chiang Mai, Le Crystal has stood the test of time, and still serves amazing food after over a decade of service. Sitting next to the peaceful Ping River, the wooden house was built to include an impeccable restaurant complete with a wine cellar. The large glass windows showcase the outdoor garden leading to the river's edge and the high ceiling creates a spacious ambience not found in many restaurants.

Le Crystal has been voted by Tatler magazine as one of Thailand's best restaurants many times and if you value high quality dishes and great service, a visit to Le Crystal is a must. The menu includes the finest French and international delights, from beef bourguignon and escargot, to foie gras and lobster. There is also an extensive wine list to match every dish on the menu and the staff are extremely knowledgeable with suitable pairings. Le Crystal is considered the best of French cuisine in Chiang Mai and a wonderful place to have a romantic dinner.

www.lecrystalrestaurant.com/en/home/
Open: 18:00 - 22:30
Location: 74/2 Paton Road, Paton
Tel: +66 (0) 53 872 890-1

THE SERVICE 1921

The Service 1921 is a classy colonial themed bar and restaurant on the grounds of the Anantara Chiang Mai Resort. Originally built in 1921 by the British government, this was the first location of the British consulate in Chiang Mai. It's no longer the consulate, but the building has still kept its stylish British interior and now serves as a restaurant fit for James Bond. Guests are escorted by ladies dressed in 1920s outfits to dark teak tables, and low lighting adds to the secretive feel. The menus at The Service 1921 come in top secret envelopes and the menu is stamped with 'For your eyes only'. There are different menus depending on the time of day you arrive, with dinner offering the best options.

The Service 1921 is a good place to try out some special Thai dishes, which are hard to find elsewhere. For example, the menu features Tom Sab Nua (Northern soup with braised beef knuckle), grilled eggplant, and crab meat salad. In addition to the restaurant, The Service 1921 has a vintage bar salon which offers an impressive wine list of old and new world wines, rare spirits sourced from the best distilleries in the world, and Cuban cigars for those who want to wrap up a meal in the men's room (now renamed the whiskey tasting room and suitable for women also). For those who wish to dine in private, there is a secret dining room behind the door hidden within a large bookshelf. It's so secretive that diners never guess the bookshelf is actually a door and so are always surprised when it opens. The Service 1921 is the perfect place to be transported back to colonial times.

www.chiang-mai.anantara.com/the-service-1921-restaurant-bar/

CUISINE DE GARDEN

Cuisine De Garden is a a relatively unknown gem of a restaurant located about 20 minutes south of the old city in Hang Dong. While the restaurant is far away, it is well worth the adventure to taste some of Chef Leelawat Mankongtiphan's enchanting dishes. Each item on the menu comes expertly presented on the plate and this is food worthy of photographing and savouring. The menu is predominantly French, with dishes such as duck, scallops and foie gras, but Leelawat changes the menu every three to four months so there is always something new to try. The restaurant itself has a simple but elegant design and would fit perfectly into any European capital. If you are a fine dining enthusiast then Cuisine De Garden is not to be missed.

Open: 11:30 -14:00 and 18:00 – 22:00
Location: 108, San Phak Wan
Tel: +66 (0) 53 441 599

THAI CUISINE

With its endless variety, flavours, colour and uniqueness, Thai cuisine is often ranked as one of the best (if not the best) in the world. There is something for everyone, from sweet to sour, mild, healthy or spicy. If you enjoy spicy food then you are in for a lot of chilli. There are also lots of options for those who don't enjoy spicy food, so don't be scared to experiment, just learn the phrase 'mai phedt'.

Dishes you must try in Chiang Mai include:

Khao Soi - yellow egg noodles, pickled cabbage, a leg of chicken covered in a rich soupy curry and topped with deep fried crispy noodles. One of the best dishes in Thailand.

Hunglay Curry - another rich, northern curry with a tamarind and shrimp paste base. Packed with slow cooked pork, the curry is somewhat oily but perfect with rice.

Sai Oua - Northern sausage filled with a mixture of pork, dried chilli, garlic, herbs and spices.

Nam Prig Ong/Num - two fiery dips that are popular in the north. Made from a mixture of red or green chilli, mashed into a sauce, these should be avoided by all but the brave. The tips are eaten with steamed vegetables, grilled pork and sticky rice.

TRY THAI IN STYLE

LE GRAND LANNA

For those who want to delve into classic Northern Thai dishes, Le Grand Lanna offers endless choices to explore. With a menu over 10 pages long, Le Grand Lanna attempts to serve up the best dishes Thailand has to offer. Try the green curry with succulent beef and eggplant, creamy red curry with fresh tiger prawns or spicy pomelo salad with dried coconut and prawns. The menu is so extensive that it is advisable to share a range of different dishes, as is normal in Thailand. Order four or five dishes for the table and your own rice, then sample to add variety to your meal. Le Grand Lanna is set in a beautiful salon filled with local treasures and every evening from 19:30 there is a cultural performance including traditional Lanna music and dance.

http://www.dharadhevi.com/EN/Dining/5
Open: 11:30 - 14:30 and 18:00 - 22:30
Location: Dhara Dhevi Hotel, 51/4 Moo 1, Chiang Mai-Sankampaeng Road
Tel: 053 888 888

RIM TAI KITCHEN

A uniquely novel way to experience Thai cuisine up close and personal. Set in the chef's kitchen, this ten course meal offers guests the opportunity to combine an exclusive dinner with a chance to sit and learn with an expert Thai chef as she whips up exotic dishes right before your eyes. Located at the Four Seasons resort in Mae Rim, which is nestled in the lush Mae Sa Valley, this two-hour demonstration meal allows guests to sample some amazing Thai dishes, as well as sip local Thai beers, wines and local spirits. The Rim Tai Kitchen chef's table experience runs Monday to Saturday starting at 7 pm and can host up to 12 guests. Booking ahead is advised to guarantee a place at this popular event.

www.fourseasons.com/chiangmai/dining/
Open: Daily at 19:00
Location: 502 Moo 1, Mae Rim-Samoeng Old Road
Tel: +66 (0) 53 298 181

SLEE BANYAN AT THE SIRIPANNA RESORT

The Slee Banyan restaurant is well known as one of the best luxury buffets in town. The international restaurant offers both lunch and dinner feasts every day, with the Sunday three hour lunch being the pinnacle dining experience here. Choose to sit under the revered Banyan tree in the garden or indoors with the Thai inspired decoration and sample some of the delights of Thai cuisine. The busy weekday buffets offer an innovative take on local dishes, as well as a range of western favourites like pizza, pasta, and bread. There are also Thai and Chinese favourites like spring rolls and dim sum, and the delicious dessert counter to seal the meal. The evening buffet has even more delights to offer, with fresh sashimi, sushi, salads, as well as a large selection of Thai dishes. The evening buffet is a wonderful way to sample a large selection of Thai curries without ordering whole plates.

Every evening features the 'dish of the day', which is a live show of a popular dish by a chef. The dish of the day ranges from elaborate soups and stir fries to tacos and steaks. Finally, the Sunday lunch offers all of the above as well as the freshest 'seafood on ice'. Carefully sourced and flown up the same morning from the gulf of Thailand, the seafood complements the elaborate Japanese selection, expansive range of barbeque, Thai dishes and western comforts. To aid digestion, on Sundays there is also a live Jazz band under the Banyan tree playing smooth sounds into the restaurant. Come to each and every meal hungry, as you will need the space to sample all the choices, and attached to the restaurant is a cocktail bar with great value for money drinks.

www.siripanna.com/dining-chiang-mai.html

RUEN TAMARIND RESTAURANT

Part of the beautiful Tamarind Village Resort in the old city of Chiang Mai, Ruen Tamarind restaurant serves up some great Thai and northern Thai food as well as international options. Choose to sit indoors in the simple and elegant dining room, or near the pool terrace to enjoy the garden area. Try the Snakehead Fish with a spicy dip, Hanglee curry (a warm pork and ginger fusion), green jackfruit curry (a rare specialty in Chiang Mai) or yam sanut, a salad mixed in a slightly spicy chilli dressing.

www.tamarindvillage.com/en/dining.php
Location: 50/1 Rajdamnoen Road
Tel: +66 (0) 53 418 897-9

SAENKHAM TERRACE

Saenkham Terrace is a Thai restaurant with great views of the mountains and rice paddies where their rice comes from. The interiour of the restaurant is simple and stylish and their menu features a whole range of popular Thai dishes. Try the Northern dish khao soi (noodle curry) or sweet and sour stir fry in a taro birds shaped nest. Saenkham Terrace is a little out of the city but well worth the drive for the atmosphere, views and fine cuisine.

www.saenkhamterrace.com
Open: 11:00 -22:00
Location: 199/163 clubhouse Baan Nai Fan, Mae Hia
Tel: +66 (0) 53 838 990

THE RIVER MARKET

The River Market restaurant is set in a beautiful wooden building with a garden area leading right up to the Ping River's edge. The building showcases a combination of Lanna, Burmese and colonial style architecture and features a high ceiling to keep the building cool even on the hottest of days. The menu at the River Market offers a large selection of seasonal Thai and seafood, prepared by expert chefs and the presentation of food here is equally as important as the quality of the ingredients. The terrace at the River Market is a great place for a romantic dinner, complete with views of the river and neighbouring Iron bridge. The bar stocks a wide selection of drinks including imported wine and beers to complement any meal.

www.therivermarket.com
Open: 10:30 -23:30
Location: 33-12 Charoenprathet Road, Chan Klan
Tel: +66 (0) 53 234 493

TRADITIONAL AND LOCAL THAI

TRADITIONAL KHANTOKE DINNER

The Khantoke Dinner at the Old Chiang Mai Cultural Center is based around the traditional Thai dinner and dancing show. The Khantoke dinner guests sit on bamboo mats or pillows on the floor and are served a selection of Northern Thai food to share with other guests at the table. The food includes a rich chicken curry and a Burmese style pork curry, fried chicken, sticky rice, vegetables with a spicy chilli dip and the Northern delicacy of deep fried pork skin. While you sit and sample a variety of Thai delights, Traditional Thai dances are performed on stage, including sword dancing and a popular drum performance. The Khantoke Dinner is a popular cultural event and a good way to see traditional performances, which are becoming increasingly rare. The Old Chiang Mai Cultural Center also has nightly Thai Boxing shows the watch over dinner.

www.oldchiangmai.com
Location: 185/3 Thipanet Road
Tel: +66 (0) 53 202 9935

TONG TEM TEH

Tucked in a quiet soi off of Nimmanhaemin Road, Tong Tem Teh is one of Chiang Mai's must visit restaurants - especially for visitors on holiday. While Tong isn't exactly fine dining, it is still worth mentioning because it is one of the best places to sample Northern cuisine. The restaurant and bar is open air and occupies a small lot in the Nimmanhaemin area. The menu is in Thai with a simplified English translation, so it is recommended to go with Thai friends who can order for you. If you are an adventurous foodie, try the Grilled Pork Neck, Nam Prig Ong (which is a Chiang Mai special chili dip), Gaeng Hanglee (pork stew) or the Spicy Chicken Curry – but be aware most items are really spicy. Wash all of the spice down with some Thai beer and deep-fried chicken wings. The menu is extensive and it's a good idea to order a few different dishes to share. The spice might not sound too appetizing, but the daily line outside the door states otherwise – be prepared to wait for up to an hour for a table. The authentic Northern Thai food at Tong is definitely worth the wait.

Hours: 17:00 - midnight
Location: Nimmanhemin Road, Soi 13
Tel: +66 (0) 53 22 2207

HUEN PHEN

A restaurant famous for its Khao Soi in the daytime, and quaint atmosphere in the evenings. There is a daytime canteen style restaurant, and a smaller, multi-roomed restaurant with wooden decoration and antique decoration, only open in the evenings. Both parts of Huen Phen are so popular that in high season, Thai's and tourists both queue for a table. In the daytime Khao Soi is the most popular dish, but they also serve jackfruit salad and fish with sweet basil steamed in banana leaf. In the evenings there is a full menu of popular Thai dishes, as well as the famous Khao Soi.

Open: 8:30- 16:00 and 17:00 -22:00
Location: Rachamanka Road
Tel: +66 (0) 52 814 548

HOT CHILLI

A bright, sensual restaurant a few streets from Thapae Road, Hot Chilli is a beautiful introduction to Thai food in a lavish style. The restaurant has swinging seats, plush pillows and red and pink decor. A sight for jet lagged eyes. While the restaurant doesn't look 'traditionally Thai' their menu features all the popular dishes, with Pad Thai, grilled fish and Massaman curry being some of the most popular options. Hot Chilli can feel a little touristy if this isn't your first time in Thailand, but for beginners it is a nice introduction to Thai food.

Open: 10:00 - 23:30
Location: Rachadamnoen Road
Tel: +66 (0) 53 278 814

DASH

Set in a large wooden house with outdoor seating, Dash restaurant is a firm favourite of visitors to Chiang Mai for its amazing Thai food. Set over two floors, with an air conditioned room in the back and lots of space in the garden, Dash has space even during the busiest of times. Every evening there is a live band which adds to the exciting atmosphere of the place. The restaurant also runs a cooking course so if you enjoy the food, ask about learning how to cook their speciality dishes. The hunglay curry, papaya salad and Tom Yum are popular favourites at Dash.

Open: 9:00- 00:00
Location: Moon Muang Road, soi 3
Tel: +66 (0) 53 279 230

LEMONGRASS RESTAURANT

One of the most popular restaurants for tourists wanting to try Thai food, Lemongrass is very close to the Night Bazaar and Loi Kroh Road. The walls have been graffitied with reviews from customers over the years in various languages. Expect a backpacker vibe, with no air-conditioning but cheap and good quality food to make up for the venue. The menu is extensive and has almost every Thai dish, including some rarer norther dishes. Try to save space for dessert as they also offer fried bananas with ice cream or banana pancakes.

Open: 16:00 - 00:00
Location: Loi Kroh Road, towards the river
Tel: +66 (0) 85 757 6337

STREET FOOD

Visitors cannot come to Thailand without trying street food at least once. Despite the usual proximity to traffic, and the basic, plastic tables, street food in Thailand is delicious - perhaps more so than most regular restaurants. Since most menus will be in Thai, choose a street stall that looks good, point to what other customers are eating and then sit down and wait for your surprise meal. A good place to start is noodle soup, which will not be spicy. On average street food costs 30-40 Baht, so if you don't like your meal you at least got the experience of street side dining. Thai Street Food is a great book to learn more about Thailand's culinary tradition.

CHIANG MAI GATE

Head to the south gate in the old city at sunset and you will see a market devoted to street food. From soups, curries and rice dishes, to grilled meat on a stick, Chiang Mai sausage and fresh fruit smoothies, this market is ideal for beginners.

Open: Daily 18:00 - 23:00
Location: Chaing Mai Gate, Bumrung Buri Road

SUNDAY WALKING STREET MARKET

The Sunday night market is another great spot to sample street delights. While the main focus of the Sunday night market is shopping for hand-made handicrafts, intertwined between the stalls are countless street food delicacies to nibble while you shop. Wat Phan On is affectionately nicknamed as the 'food temple' because every Sunday a whole variety of street stalls set up in the picnic area for shoppers. Come to the market hungry as there is so much good food to be found.

Open: Sundays 17:00- 00:00
Location: Ratchadamneon Road

PLOEN RUDEE NIGHT MARKET

A daily night market with a nice variety of street stalls and food trucks. There is more western food here compared to the Sunday Night Market, but also lots of Thai options. The food stalls are located around the outside of the market, with tables, chairs and haystacks to sit on in the middle. There is also a stage with nightly music from local bands. This is the prettier part of the Night Bazaar area.

Open: daily 17:30 - 23:30
Location: Chang Klan Road

CAFES & HIGH TEA

Chiang Mai is more of a cafe city than a bar city, which is why it is important for coffee and high tea lovers to know the best spots in town. High tea has always been a popular activity all over the world, and the following hotels do it delightfully. Coffee however, is trickier to execute, yet there are many skilled baristas that sought training abroad and have brought back the art of a good cup of coffee to Chiang Mai. Most of the world doesn't know that both tea and coffee is grown in Northern Thailand and exported. Starbucks buys thousands of kilos of Thai robusta yearly, so it's wise to pick up some beans direct from the source while you are here.

DOPPIO RISTR8TO

No, that's not a typo, the eight really is in their name, and all the drink prices end in eight also, e.g. a cappuccino is 88 Baht. The name is nowhere near as memorable as the coffee here, which has won numerous awards across the world. The owner worked for many years in Australia, perfecting the art of making double ristretto shots, as well as exquisite latte art. Today only the rist8tto's remain as the cafe is too busy for staff to spend time drawing on latte foam. This was the first speciality coffee shop to hit Chiang Mai, and its original location on Nimmanhaemin Road is always packed, from 7:08 until 18:08 when it closes. Note, there is only coffee, decaf coffee and hot chocolate on the menu so if you are a tea drinker then consider visiting a different cafe.

www.ristr8to-coffee-chiangmai.com

ASAMA

A small and hard to find coffee shop far from the city centre, Asama is often sought out only by coffee enthusiasts. Asama's owner Mook is one of Thailand's judges for the national barista championships and serves up her own blend of coffee from local and imported beans. The hidden away cafe is a small room (the coffee machine takes up most of the room) with some outdoor seating and a great view of Doi Suthep mountain over a small pond. As well as traditional favourites with the option of double shots, Asama cafe also has some interesting options including a sparkling espresso and a black and white anti gravity coffee.

www.facebook.com/AsamaCafe

AKHA AMA

A small, quaint social enterprise that is truly unique to Chiang Mai, Akha Ama cafe is a great cafe to visit and explore coffee from the region. All of the coffee comes from the founder's home village; an Akha village two hours north of Chiang Mai and has been grown, harvested and roasted by the small enterprise itself. All proceeds go back into helping the village and community, so by drinking coffee here you are helping a small hill tribe village. They do inspirational and educational coffee tours in early December so check their website for information on the dates.

www.akhaama.com

WOO CAFE AND GALLERY

A wonderful, bright and vibrant space, Woo cafe is a feast for the eyes and stomach. Not only is the cafe filled with flowers, leafy plants art and tea, but the menu is also filled with delicious food. The cakes are also to die for, each baked fresh daily and displayed in front of the till. Above the cafe is a gallery space with two rooms of local artist pieces.

www.woochiangmai.com

FABB COFFEE ROASTERS

Fabb Coffee Roasters is also a little out of town, but very close to Asama cafe. The cafe originated in Bangkok but the owner, Janejira, moved to Chiang Mai for a slower pace of life. Janejira is the first Thai to have been trained as a SCAE (Specialty Coffee Association of Europe) trainer and offers roasting, brewing and barista training at various levels if you want to learn more about coffee. Her cafe is part coffee adventure, part relaxed lounge area and the seating room has an impressive book selection and even features a grand piano for use by those who can play well. The cafe offers over 65 different bean origins from as far flung as Yemen, Papua New Guinea, Burma and Peruv, as well as more local Thai and Laotian beans. There is also a full menu of food available for those who have worked up an appetite from too much coffee.

www.facebook.com/fabb.cafeandbistro

TITA GALLERY

With a stunning backdrop of mountains and nature stopping right on the doorstep,

Tita Gallery is the perfect place to get away from the city. From the Four Seasons Mae Rim Resort it's less than a 5-minute walk away and yet the elegant first floor with its fine details and rare Thai artwork you will feel as if you've never left your luxury hotel. The coffee comes from a local hill tribe and some of the best cakes in Northern Thailand can be found here. Tita tries to remain environmentally friendly in their actions, so they don't run air conditioning and source as much organic produce as possible. This attention to nature allows customers to feel more connected to nature too. Open air seating is cool, shaded by trees and umbrellas, and the indoor area is built Thai style to allow good ventilation. The perfect place to curl up and read a book on a rainy day.

www.facebook.com/TitaGallery/

DHARA DHEVI CAKE SHOP

Located just outside the main entrance of the Dhara Dhevi is the Kad Dhara Shopping Village, which houses the delicious Dhara Dhevi Cake Shop. A classy, Victorian tea salon, the Cake Shop has a range of homemade pastries, cakes, and serve a fine selection of quality teas and a uniquely sourced coffee blend. The homemade macaroons served at the Cake Shop are famous all over Asia and many visitors to Chiang Mai make the journey out the Dhara Dhevi just for them. Because they have become so popular the Cake Shop has expanded and now includes locations in Bangkok, although they are freshest at their source - in the Cake shop overlooking the quaint courtyard. The Dhara Dhevi Cake Shop also serves high tea daily from 12 - 6 pm, which includes unlimited tea and a mixture of 25 tasty treats - including macaroons. Not to be missed!

http://www.dharadhevi.com/EN/Dining/2

ANANTARA HIGH TEA

Formally the British consulate building, and then luxury hotel The Chedi, the resort finally lies in the hands of the Anantara luxury chain. The hotel boasts impressive colonial architecture and peaceful views over the Ping riverside. The famous high tea at the Anantara brings in the historical aspect of high tea ceremony with guests sitting in the same location as former British royalty decades ago. The tower features high tea favourites including scones with clotted cream, macarons, decadent chocolate cake, as well as savory snacks created by the former Indian head chef. Imported teas and coffee are served with the tower of English delights, and high tea runs from 2pm - 6pm, with Saturday and Sundays offering an even more impressive version of the high tea ceremony. Champagne can be added upon request for celebratory occasions.

www.anantara.com/thailand

137 PILLARS HIGH TEA

Keeping with the history of the 137 Pillars house, no visit here would be complete without a traditional high tea experience, which date back to the first residents on the property. The classic high tea set at the 137 Pillars house is served either under the imposing banyan trees in the manicured lawn area, or in the parlor area of the house. The parlor area is ideal for relaxing with friends over high tea, with plush armchairs, cozy day beds complete with azure blue mosquito nets, a stunning view of the green wall and countless interesting Thai sculptures dotted around the lounge. High tea can also be served surrounded by books within the Jack Bains bar which is air conditioned and perfect for lounging and nibbling for hours.

The high tea set allows guests to choose from a variety of finely sourced teas or coffee, and each guests gets their own designer teapot which is refilled often by diligent staff. The three tiered cake stand is delivered and packed with sweet and savory delicacies. High tea in a former colonial building sets a high standard for the afternoon and for the treats. Scones are a must, and served with real clotted cream and strawberry jam, while the lower layers of the stand hold quaint egg sandwiches and sweet lemon tarts. The mango panna cotta adds an Asian twist to a traditional tea set, and at the top of the cake stand lay delicate lavender macaroons topped with gold. Sweet treats don't come more luxurious than this. For special occasions high tea can be ordered with Sparkling Prosecco or sabered champagne, a good option for honeymooners. And for those who are looking for the ultimate in luxury combine high tea with a trip to the 137 Pillars spa. High tea at the 137 Pillars house is the perfect way to spend an afternoon and a must for any visitors to Chiang Mai as high tea can be combined with a glimpse of Chiang Mai's history and the beauty of the 137 Pillars House property.

www.137pillarschiangmai.com/en/dining/#afternoontea

NAKARA JARDIN

Nakara Jardin sits serenely next to the Ping Nakara Boutique hotel and overlooks the riverside and Ping River. The perfect setting for high tea, Nakara Jardin is an open, lush garden welcoming guests with a Thai smile and a touch of French elegance. The high tea set has been designed by a former Le Cordon Bleu graduate and offers a mixture of French and English delights. There is also a Thai style high tea available in the Ping Nakara hotel itself, so depending on which culture you wish to taste choose accordingly. There is also a full dessert and coffee menu for those not wishing to have high tea.

www.pingnakara.com/nakara_jardin

VIENG JOOM ON

A beautiful teahouse on the bank of the Ping river, Vieng Joom On is a good high tea alternative. Locally famous for its unique blends of exotic tea, elaborate cakes and macaroons, it is becoming 'the' place to visit for those with a sweet tooth. The building is impossible to miss with bright pink exterior walls and inside the colour continues. The bright tea room has a wall of white metal tins containing loose leaf tea, while the room is a bright airy mix of different tables and comfy chairs. There are indoor hanging plants and on a cool day guests can sit outside on the patio overlooking the river. There is food available as well as sweet treats, and if you really enjoy desserts then Vieng Joom On has it's own version of high tea, although instead of scones, guests are treated to fresh regional fruit. A trip to Vieng Joom On can be remembered by buying some tea to take home as you leave. Vieng Joom On has such a relaxed atmosphere that you will probably linger longer than you planned.

Open: 10:00 – 19:00
Address: 53 Charoenraj Road, Wat Kate
Tel: +66 (0)53 303 113

PUNNA CAFÉ

A high tea with a twist, Punna café mixes the concept of traditional high tea with a vast array of Thai food and desserts to create an afternoon banquet of sweet and savory finger food. The high tea is set in an air conditioned teak paneled lounge area with a bar, and because their high tea is not as well-known as some of the other hotels chances are you may have the whole room to yourselves. The staff are dressed in traditional Thai style outfits and Punna Cafés version of high tea feels less colonial and more an example of how Thai people love to enjoy food. In Thai history tea a light meal was popular among the Thai Royal Court and Punna Café have tried to maintain the culture and serve up dishes which take time to prepare and are artworks within themselves.

The experience starts with choosing the tea from an array of classic teas, before a tiered high tea stand is brought in. The top two layers display beautiful examples of Thai jellied desserts and coconut rice balls, while the bottom is packed with delightful little sandwiches almost too beautiful to eat. However the high tea stand is just the beginning. The staff continue to bring in elaborate dishes of food, from chilled multi coloured vegetables in a bowl to canapés of fried sticky rice and chicken. A stand of carved fruit is one of the prettiest dishes on the table, with papaya carved into leaves and watermelons into hearts. The final dish to be brought is a generous helping of mango and sticky rice, and once space is made on the table for the traditional dessert, the high tea feast can begin.

www.puripunn.com/dinning-spa/

BARS / NIGHTLIFE

Chiang Mai doesn't have the same night life as the rest of Thailand. In fact, Chiang Mai doesn't have much of a nightlife at all. In recent years, the local authorities attempted to close all bars and clubs at midnight, in an effort to maintain the sleepy, relaxed atmosphere of the city. This worked surprisingly well, and although there are a few spots open past midnight (for example the rooftop complex at Maya mall), most of the city goes to bed early. However, if you want to explore Chiang Mai nights then there are still a few interesting places open to visit. In order to combat the early curfew, nightlife in Chiang Mai starts earlier. There are many spots to watch the sunset over a cocktail or cold beer, with many beautiful rooftop bars offering beautiful views of Wat Doi Suthep and Doi Pui. Live music is also incredibly popular in Chiang Mai, with the North Gate Jazz Bar often attracting world class Jazz musicians on their holidays.

Rise Bar at Akyra Manor

NORTH GATE JAZZ BAR

On Tuesday nights you never know what you are going to get as the North Gate Jazz bar opens the floor to all musicians to jam. Sometimes laid back soulful music, other times an enlivening rap and hip hop vibe comes forth organically. Then there are the days where it is so busy that jazz enthusiasts stand out in the road, slowing and almost stopping traffic in their excitement and desire to dance. By far the best jazz club in town, if not in Thailand, and lovers of live music must visit this place. While Tuesdays are packed, North Gate Jazz bar is open daily and usually two bands play every evening starting at 9 pm. On quieter days, visitors get to soak up the atmosphere and ambience of the modest venue.

Open daily from 19:00
Location: 91/1-2, Si Phum Road

BOYS BLUES BAR

Another hot spot for live music lovers is Boys Blues Bar. Hovering in a venue above the Night Bazaar, this buzzing night bazaar spot belts out the blues six nights a week (except Sundays when its closed). Located on the second story overlooking the maze of stalls, Boy and friends perform a mixture of classic blues and contemporary live music. Mondays are jam night so if you fancy joining in just follow the soulful music drifting out over the night bazaar.

www.boybluesbar.com
Open: 19:00 - 01:00
Location: In the Kalare Centre (near the food hall) at the Night Bazaar

MAYA ROOFTOP

The Maya shopping mall rooftop holds five of the coolest bars in Chiang Mai, and offers stunning city wide vistas and the perfect view of the sun setting behind the mountain. The mall is conveniently located on Huey Kaew Road close to Nimmanhaemin Road and open later than the midnight curfew, so this is the place to go if you want to party!

Of the five bars, Myst is usually the busiest. Originating in the trendy Thonglor area of Bangkok, Myst invaded Chiang Mai bringing a wide range of elaborate cocktails, shisha pipes, live music and DJs and the high society crowd of Chiang Mai. The most famous drink at Myst is the rainbow shot mix which is a selection of 7 different coloured shots with dry ice added, meaning the shots look like they are giving off steam. The Buckets Siamese Bar allows you to experience the traditional way of drinking in Thailand - cocktails in a plastic bucket filled with straws or a tower of beer shared on the table. While the idea of the bucket originated from the full moon parties on Koh Phangan, this bar makes the bucket a novelty and serves up expertly crafted cocktails in the plastic container. Many places in Thailand promote the beer tower as it lets you help yourself to beer 'on tap' when your glass is empty. Surreal drinking options but fun all the same. Your Bar is another rooftop place serving up interesting cocktails such as 'lost in paradise' and 'midnight in Paris', and the band competes with Myst for who is the loudest. The rooftop is open from 4pm but the bars don't start opening until 6pm onwards - just in time for sunset. Most of the customers are either Thai or local expats and it is a great place to glimpse local life in Chiang Mai.

Open: 18:00 -01:00
Location: Maya Shopping Mall, corner of Huey Kaew Road and Nimman Road intersection

RISE ROOFTOP BAR

If you are looking to party in style then Nimmanhaemin is the area to go, and Rise Rooftop bar is the place to start. From the 8th floor of the five star luxurious hotel, the rooftop bar is open to the public for both drinks and dinner. Offering spectacular vistas over the varied rooftops of Nimmanhaemin road and the Doi Pui mountain, Rise bar is the perfect place to watch sunset with a glass of champagne or a classic cocktail. With expert mixology bartenders and an extensive wine list offering wines from around the world including Thailand there is no better place than Rise to relax and start your evening in style. Rise Rooftop bar offers a daily happy hour from 5.30 -6.30pm where you can sip your drink in the glass sided pool. Alternatively sink into their plush sofas by the pool and try their signature Italics cocktail which includes vodka, buffalo milk and a drop of cinnamon syrup.

Open: 15:00 - 01:00
Location: 22/2 Nimmanhaemin Road, Soi 9

YAYEE ROOFTOP BAR

Hotel Yayee's rooftop bar has the perfect view of the mountain for sunset. Being four floors up, and with no larger condos blocking the view, Yayee's rooftop lets you watch the busyness of Nimman, and the relaxing sunset in one view. The hotel is owned by the famous Thai actor Ananda Everigham, who occasionally hangs out on his rooftop. The bar has an interesting menu of hand crafted cocktails as well as food from the restaurant on the ground floor. Head there around 6pm for sunset and dinner.

Open: 17:00 - 00:00
Location: Nimmanhemin road, 17/5 Sainamphueng alley

RIVERSIDE BAR AND RESTAURANT

The Riverside is part bar, part restaurant, and offers great views over the Ping River as well as live music and a wide variety of Thai and western dishes on the menu. The decor inside is retro and comfortable, and lends itself to excellent acoustics for the nightly live band and after dinner atmosphere. The best time to visit is around sunset, where you can overlook the idyl River, have a cocktail or imported beer, and start to look through the extensive menu to decide the unusual Thai dish you want to try. Book in advance if you want a riverside table, as on most nights the restaurant can get busy. Alternatively, take a relaxing river cruise down the Ping River while enjoying a set dinner and a glass of wine. It's a unique way to see some of traditional life and villages which still rely on the river for sustenance.

If the Riverside Bar and Restaurant is too full, then try its neighbour, The Good View – a similar setup with a competing live music band, but a less monumental menu.

www.theriversidechiangmai.com

BEER LAB

A famous beer bar in Bangkok, Beer Lab opened in Chiang Mai to serve the increasing desire from locals to sample imported beers from around the world. Part beer garden, part sports bar, Beer Lab has a lively atmosphere and both indoor and outdoor seating depending if you want air conditioning or to watch the world go by on Nimmanhaemin Road. Their beer menu consists of over 20 pages of imported craft beer from all around the world, and the variety is impressive. From American and Australian to various European and Japanese beers, if you are looking for a well-known beer or brand, they will have it. For non-beer drinkers, Beer Lab also serves cocktails and wine.

The selection is reasonably well priced, with imported bottles starting around 200 Baht (imported beers are taxed highly in Thailand, which makes them more expensive than domestic beers). Beer Lab also has a separate, and equally large food menu comprised of great steaks, sausages and snacks, as well as a variety of Thai dishes. On Friday and Saturday nights Beer Lab is packed, but the friendly staff will always do their best to find a table for guests.

www.facebook.com/beerlabchiangmai

MIXOLOGY BAR

A cozy little bar offering a range of colourful and uniquely flavoured cocktails such as Tom Yum flavoured martini, imported beer and cider and a great view to watch the evening rush hour around the moat (which actually lasts around 20 minutes). The mixologist went to school in London to become an expert in his trade and the study pays off in the first sip. While Mixology is hard to spot and looks small from the outside, there is ample seating in the inviting bar/restaurant with lots of interesting decorations to keep your eyes busy while you wait for your drinks.

In addition to drinks, Mixology is also a great place to eat. Try their Chiang Mai burger (which replaces the burger bun with sticky rice), steak, curries and some excellent Thai-style salads.

www.facebook.com/MixologyChiangmaiBurger/

THE SERVICE 1921 BAR

A restaurant and bar situated in the old British Consulate building, this is also the place to visit if you are looking for fine wines, vintage whiskey or the more elaborate cocktails in town. Ask for Doctor X. and she will will appear at your table in a cloud of smoke, ready to mix up a cocktail to match your desires. A trained and award winning mixologist, Doctor X. has the best cocktails in Chiang Mai, if not Thailand. Meeting her is not to be missed on a visit to Chiang Mai.

http://chiang-mai.anantara.com/the-service-1921-restaurant-bar

RED ROOM WINE BAR

Not content to serve only the best food in town, the team behind David's Kitchen decided to also open a wine bar - The Red Room. Located next to David's Kitchen, the dark, richly decorated room wouldn't be out of place in Paris, and neither would the wine. There is also a range of high end spirits, and some delicious cocktails. Start at the Red Room before going to dinner, and return again after for a late night indulgence.

Open: 17.00- 00:00
Location: 113 Bamrungrad Road

WARM UP

If you are looking for nightlife in Chiang Mai, this is it. Warm Up Cafe is the city's longest running club and arguably the best. Even though the name says café, there is no tea or coffee served in this vibrant nighttime spot. Famous bands, DJs, and even the occasional Thai celebrity can be found enjoying the atmosphere in the trendy Nimmanhaemin club. The closed rooms to the back and side often offer different kinds of music, while the front of Warm Up offers a more casual sit, drink and chat vibe.

www.facebook.com/warmupcafe1999/

INFINITY

The only other 'club' in town worth noting is Infinity. Located a little off Nimmanhaemin Road, Infinity wouldn't be out of place in a European city and features live bands, a dance floor and laser lighting from the 90s in Ibiza. Most customers in infinity are dressed up, and heels and party dresses are welcomed. On the weekends Infinity gets busy, especially later in the evening as it is one of the places that stays open the longest.

www.facebook.com/infinity.chiangmai

UN IRISH PUB

While football is popular in Chiang Mai, The UN Irish Pub is the best place to catch any sporting event. From American NFL, Auzzie rules football, Ice Hockey to Rugby union or league (and even the occasional handball game), The UN Irish pub stays open late, and opens early to screen live games from across the world. If you cannot live without seeing your team win whilst on holiday, then head to the old city, grab a traditional meat pie and pint of Guinness and meet other expats or holidaymakers who cannot live without their sports. Check the UN website for latest events and fixtures.

www.unirishpub.com

SHOPPING

Bangkok is often touted as the best city for shopping in Asia because of a unique blend of brands, unique designers, boutiques and incredibly diverse tourists coming to shop in the city. However while Chiang Mai is often overlooked on a serious shoppers itinerary, is it arguably an even better spot to shop because stores focus on what they are good at producing - be it teak furniture, hand crafted parasols or intricately woven sarongs - rather than selling the latest styles. This means that most items on sale in Chiang Mai are unique to the region or country, and hold a long history dating back hundreds of years. From ancient ways of carving wood, hand weaving elaborate clothing or bags in hilltribe designs to unique beauty products made from local herbs, Chiang Mai has something different to offer even a seasoned traveller. And then there is the Sunday Walking Street - if you love to shop then visiting Asia's best market is a must.

In Chiang Mai the three best shopping areas (that aren't markets) are Nimmanhaemin Road and its soi's, Thapae Road and Phrapokklao Road in the old city. There are also a few shopping malls with brands similar to what you'd find at home (but have great air conditioning if you are in need of cooler temperatures).

Tips

- If there is no price on the item then a friendly haggle is usually welcomed. Most sellers will understand 'discount' and almost always offer one, even if it isn't much.
- Don't haggle hard as this will only offend the seller. Thailand is a friendly and hospitable place and so the friendlier you are the happier they are to deal with you.
- First sale. Most vendors believe that the first sale of the day is lucky (and opens the floodgates to more sales) so they are happy to offer you a bigger discount, especially on multiple items. Again ask about it with a smile.
- Since the average wage in Thailand is 300 Baht a day ($10 USD) or 30 Baht an hour, tips or paying full price is always appreciated. Most Thai's are aware of how much western countries earn and are always gracious when foreigners aren't haggling (except out of friendly play).

MARKETS

SUNDAY WALKING STREET

The Sunday Walking Street is a shoppers paradise. Thousands of stalls line the sides of a main road in the old city, offering some of the most unique, ornate and unusual items in the country. Vendors are ever innovative unless an item is a bestseller - like soaps, paper lantern lights, silk scarves and cotton Thai shirts. Most items are hand crafted by the seller at the stall and the quality goes above and beyond most items shop bought. But the Sunday Walking Street doesn't only sell things to buy, rather it is a cultural experience not to be missed and is interesting even for those who don't like to shop. Delicious street snacks are dotted all along the 1.5km street, as well as cultural events, live musicians, handcrafted artifacts and paintings representing Thai culture and religious life.

On most Sundays the smaller streets off Ratchadamnoen Road have stages set up for local events like traditional thai dancing, beauty pageants, live music or student recitals. Along every road of the Sunday walking street there is a sight to see or something traditional to try. The epicentre of Chiang Mai's old city becomes a giant maze of vendors, shoppers and visitors into the northern Kingdom. The market is on every Sunday and starting at thapae gate the epic night market runs west across the old city to Wat Phra Singh. The roads are closed to cars allowing for visitors to explore, and there are also street side foot massage stalls to relax while people watching.

Opening Hours: Best time to go is around 5pm before it gets busy or after 9pm (when the crowds thin)
Location: Thapae Gate, Ratchadamneon Road and Wat Phra Singh

SATURDAY WALKING STREET

Saturday's Walking Street along Wulai Road is surprisingly different from the Sunday version. While the stalls feature similar (if not the same) items, the atmosphere and set up of Saturdays Walking Street is different to the sunday version. Saturday is more about shopping so if your suitcase is already full then skip Wulai road (or just check out the night market at Chiang Mai gate for food and smoothies). If it is not high season the Saturday Night Market is not usually crowded, but during November and December the Saturday is busier than Sunday since the street in question is smaller. Local handicrafts, herbal beauty products, clothes, souvenirs, snacks, dried fruits, jewellery and even up and coming designers can be found here. Sunset is the busiest time for most shoppers, so if you want to avoid the crowds head there around 9pm.

Opening Hours: 17:00 until 23:00 (approximately), Saturday nights only
Location: Wualai Road, near the South moat of the old town

WAROROT AND THE TON LAMYAI FLOWER MARKET

Neighbouring markets, both located between the old city and the river, Warorot Market is nicknamed the 'Chinese Market' and Ton Lamyai the beautiful flower market. Ton Lamyai is open almost 24 hours and is a feast for the eyes and nose. Here you'll find some of the most amazing varieties of flowers including orchids, rare lilies, locally grown roses, fresh chrysanthemums and countless other unknown species of dazzling flowers all perched on the pavement in buckets, waiting to be moved to beautiful hotels all over Chiang Mai. The flower market is one of the most interesting markets in Chiang Mai, and definitely the best smelling, but its neighbour Warorot market is a different kind of unique. Small, hot and a little bit dirty, the Chinese market offers cheap clothing, accessories and food stuffs including the famous Chiang Mai sausage (sai oua), red and green chili dip (nam prik ong/nam prik noom) or the questionable crispy pork skin (cap moo). There are lots of stalls to try local food and just outside the market vendors sell fresh fruit by the kilo as well as fried snacks. Inside Warorot market are a host of sights and smells, and it's the perfect example of a local market. While the upper floors house cheap clothing and accessories, the ground floor allows visitors to engage all of their senses, from spicy smells to elaborate meat preparation, sounds of the vendors shouting across the market hall to try out some of the prepared food there. And once you have visited Warorot Market, return around the corner to Ton Lamyai and calm yourself with the beautiful scents and sights of bright flowers.

Open: Warorot 06:00-19:00, Ton Lamyai 24 hours
Location: Chang Moi Road to Praisani Road, close to the River

NIGHT BAZAAR

The sleazier version of a night market, the Night Bazaar is open daily, come rain or shine and offers fake versions of everything you could want. Football t-shirts, sunglasses, shoes and bags, if you are looking for a replica then the Night Bazaar will stock it. There are actually countless other items available too, including souvenirs, Chang T-shirts, copied DVDs and beach dresses. Don't expect to find ornate gifts or skilled handicrafts here, rather enjoy the market for what it is - a lot of fakes from China, and try out one of the bars or restaurants in the covered part of the Bazaar. If you feel like dabbling into the crazy nightlife of Thailand then check out the Ladyboy Cabaret show, twice a night near the food court. A colourful, frilly spectacle of performers wearing 6 inch heels and too much make up.

Open: 18:00 – 23:00 daily
Location: Intersection of Chang Khlan Road and Loi Kroh Road

ANTIQUES

Thailand has a surprising amount of antiques floating around the country, some of which make it into museums but more than not end up as cafe decoration or in showrooms waiting to be bought. Since Thailand was never colonised, many artifacts date back to the Kingdoms before Siam or have made their way across the borders from Myanmar or Cambodia shortly before wars and genocides started. While those who know what they are looking at can find antiques almost anywhere in Northern Thailand. For more cautious shoppers it's best to visit the better known boutiques first to get a feel for what's real.

THE GOLDEN TRIANGLE

The largest antique store in Chiang Mai, The Golden Triangle is aptly named since the actual triangle has a porous border with lots of antiques being smuggled into the country along with money and drugs from China. However don't be afraid of the name, rather The Golden Triangle is one of the most interesting and unusual stores in Chiang Mai. From ancient Chinese and indian pieces to British colonial and Burmese furniture, or even old Thai and Lanna artwork, this 2- hectare shop has something to interest everyone. Plan for at least an hour to wander through the different buildings in the courtyard, and even if you don't buy anything you will still learn a lot about Northern Thailand's history.

www.goldentriangle.co.th/products.html
Location: 82 Moo 1 Chiang Mai - Hod Road, Hang Dong

T. TARA COLLECTION

T. Tara Collection stocks a wide range of beautiful antiques, crafts, carvings and artworks, both Thai and imported. It's a good place to explore and the price tags suit all budgets right by the picturesque riverside. T. Tara collection has an impressively wide range of Buddha statues, all shapes and sizes, and the staff will wrap (and ship it for you) if needed.

Opening Hours: 09:00 – 19:00
Address: 78/1 Charoenprathet Road, one block away from the Iron Bridge, on the way to Night Bazaar
Tel: +66 (0) 5381 8191

NINA ANTIQUES

An Aladdin's cave of a store, Nina Antiques offers visitors some of the finest hidden gems in Thailand. Run by Italians Marisa and Angelo, husband and wife with keen eyes to spot the finest Asian antiques. With Angelo also being an expert in antique watches and jewellery, this couple are the perfect people to tour you through the history of Southeast Asia with artifacts. While the ground floor is full of unique items, the first floor is a more spacious display of imported furniture from across the world. Opium weights from Shan State in Myanmar, French carriage clocks and ornate Chinese screens are just a few of the amazing collection Nina antiques has to offer.

www.nina-antiques.com
Location: 144/3-4 Charoenprathet Road (Opposite the Anantara Hotel)
Tel : +66-053-271256

HANDICRAFTS

BOR SANG VILLAGE

Bor Sang Village is best known for their handmade parasols and handicraft specialties and is worth a visit to see the workers skills alone. The beautiful silk umbrellas are an official symbol of Chiang Mai and have become famous both in Thailand and worldwide. The umbrella village in Bor Sang is part workshop, part museum where visitors can witness and partake in the whole parasol making process. From drying the mulberry paper, to painting the final design on the silk, it's an enjoyable experience and one of the original tourist highlights of Chiang Mai. For the artistically challenged there are miniature cocktail umbrellas that can be painted on instead. The umbrella village also has a gift shop and cafe area so visitors can purchase the final products made in the village. Every January there is a village fair and festival of umbrellas celebrated here where the city comes alive with colours, music, parades and parasols.

Open: 8:00 - 17:00
Location: highway 1014, San Kamphaeng District

HANDICRAFT HIGHWAY

The road to Sam Kampaeng district (or Highway 1006) is nicknamed the handicraft highway because of the high concentration of silk, umbrella and handicraft factories and workshops alongside the road. As well as the parasol village of Bor Sang (located just off highway 1006) there are also many shops and warehouses selling fine handicrafts. Look out for shops selling wooden lacquerware painted with shiny black lacquer and oriental designs, or the workshops housing skilled craftsmen carving ornate woodcarvings of religious beings and historical fairytales. Also along the road you will see countless outlets of Celadon ceramics, the finest kind of Thai ceramics, glazed with faint blue and light green tones and the knowledge of the blending of local clay and ash being passed along the generations. Silk and stunningly designed textiles can also be found along the highway 1006. Even before Jim Thompson arrived in Thailand the country was known for its soft and pure silk, and the clothing and textile shops in Sam Kampaeng showcase a range of ethnic designs, handwoven items and most places will even tailor items to fit perfectly.

BAN TAWAI

South of the city is Ban Tawai, one of the largest wholesale stores for handicrafts. Ban Tawai stocks an extensive range of furniture, ceramics, wood carvings, sculptures and even some ancient antiques. An OTOP (one tambon, one product) tourism village for its unique wood carving culture, maintenance of their heritage and protection of local wisdom, and at one time it was the largest handicraft village in Thailand. While some of the gigantic wooden tables are too heavy to lift by hand, there are countless smaller items to take home as memories in ban Tawai. There is even a range of clothing, bags, jewellery and carpets for those who want something easy to transport. And if you have your heart set on the elaborate wooden table then the staff at Ban Tawai can make sure that it gets to your home somehow.

Location: 90 Moo 2 ban-Tawai Khun Khong, Hang Dong
Tel: 081 882 4882

CLOTHING & TEXTILES

STUDIO NAENNA

The main gallery and weaving studio of Studio Naenna is hidden away from the crowds and only those fortunate to hear about it can visit. Nestled at the food of Doi Pui Mountain and about 15 minutes away from Nimmanhaemin road, it's best to visit Studio Naenna as more than just a shopping experience. Rather visit the studio as an experience to learn how fabric is dyed (by hand of course), how to create different dye colours and also to see backstrap loom weaving in action. Founded back in 1988 by Patricia Cheesman, an expert in Thai textiles and antiques and a lecturer at Chiang Mai University, she wanted to ensure that the local and complex skills of weaving was protected. Under her assistance over 2000 year old techniques have been preserved and young weavers trained in the ancient art. Check their website www.studio-naenna.com for up and coming workshops. The studio creates unique textiles for modern living, from clothing, scarves and accessories, Studio Naenna is a learning experience and also a place to thank for ensuring that the ancient art of weaving survives in the future. For those short on time, or who just want to shop, then head to the Adorn with Studio Naenna shop on Soi 1 of Nimmanhaemin road. Their city branch offers a range of items made in the studio.

Open: 9:00 - 17:00
Location:Nimmanhaemin Road, Soi 1
Tel: 053 226 042

DOI TUNG LIFESTYLE

The Doi Tung Development Project was set up by the late Princess Mother, Princess Srinagarindra, to carry out development activities so that the quality of life of Thailand's ethnic minorities in the Doi Tung area could be improved. The Foundation's central mission is *to keep the Princess Mother's development legacy alive to benefit as many people as possible and to inspire new generations to be responsible, engaged citizens.* The result was a chain of cafes and shops showcasing products made in the Doi Tung area. All items, from kitchenware to clothing, scarves and housewares, are made from the finest materials and have stunning designs - fit for royalty. Items are tax free for travellers but you have to reclaim the tax at the airport.

Open: 10:00 - 20:00
Location: Nimmanhaemin Rd opposite Soi 1, and in Chiang Mai airport in front of the domestic departure gate.
Tel: 053 217 981

VILA CINI

One of the best shops to buy silk and local textiles in Chiang Mai, Vila Cini has sourced the finest materials to save visitors to Chiang Mai time - everything they sell has a unique charm to it, and all housed in a classic teak house near the river. Vila Cini sells more than just textiles, they stock a range of home accessories, bags and even jewellery. Around the corner from the main shop is the new Vila Cini Village, a collection of buildings that house wood carvings, household decorations and some selections of local artisans (including **ROC** jewellery). The village also has a workshop and antique museum to explore.

Location: 30 Charoenrajd Road, Wat Gate, Chiang Mai
Open: 10:00 - 20:30
Tel: 053 246 246

WEAVE

Weave is a wonderful clothing and accessory shop set up primarily as an income generation project to allow ethnic minorities within Thailand to support themselves through their craftsmanship skills. WEAVE stands for the Women's Education for advancement and Empowerment and aims to empower indigenous women, who tend to be marginalised and often struggle to meet their basic needs within Thailand. WEAVE has an intriguing shop in Chiang Mai filled with completely handmade crafts, clothes and accessories by refugees or disadvantaged women in Thailand. Each item in the shop comes with a tag explaining which community made the item, so you know exactly where the money is going. WEAVE itself is a non-profit and their shops serve as a way to connect shoppers with skilled craftswomen across Thailand. Weave offers training to at risk groups and encourages leadership and share skills within communities to increase their outreach opportunities. While Chiang Mai is their main branch, WAVE also has a popular branch in the Thai border town of Mae Sot.

Open: 10:00 - 17:00
Location: 17/4 Sirimangkalanjarn Road, Soi 7
Tel: 080 499 8489

GINGER

A colourful treasure trove of eye catchingly beautiful items, Thai brand Ginger offers a mixture of Danish and Asian design to fall in love with. The colours are bright, bold and not for the feeble as they will make heads turn, however the design and cut will make you feel like a superstar. Located at The House, which is a restaurant, cafe and shopping combination, Ginger is a collection of different rooms filled with interesting and unusual items. Originally known for its homeware and furniture, it has evolved into offering a range of women and men's clothing, kidswear and accessories. Shopping here is fun for the whole family as children can get lost in the bright and cheerful rooms. The accessories for women are almost the best part of the shop, with many featuring feathers, pearls and fake diamonds. The best way to describe Ginger is Cath Kidson on acid.

Open: 10:00 - 22:00
Location: 199 Moonmuang Road, Si Phum
Tel: 053 419 011

MESIMU

Another brand that feels like the eccentric cousin of Cath Kidston is Mesimu. A local brand focusing on handmade bags, women's and children's clothing and shoes – all with colour. One of brightest brands on Nimmanhaemin road, you can't miss the electric green shop with window displays of colour. What is impressive about Mesimu is their ethical policy ensuring everything from the staff employed to the laborers making their bags (and everything in between) is as fair as possible. Anyone who loves bright colours or floral patterns will love Mesimu.

Open: 10:30 – 20:00, Sat/ Sun 11:00 – 20:00
Address: 4-4/1 Nimmanhaemin Road

JEWELLERY

ERANYARA

A truly talented jewellery maker and one of the nicest boutiques in Chiang Mai, Eranyara is a place to visit if your neck is feeling empty. Handmade and unique pieces designed by local designers Rakchanok, each necklace has been created from local stones and regional gems to create truly international creations. Wear these items with pride as each one has been painstakingly sourced and crafted by Rakchanok. Her shop is located on the Sunday walking street, but it's best to go in the week as the shop feels more like an art gallery, with stylish pieces to adore.

www.eranyara.com
Open: 10:00 - 20:00
Location: Rachadamnoen Road
Tel: 088 262 0163

NOVA JEWELLERY

In the middle of one of Chiang Mai's shopping districts, Thapae Road, Nova Jewellery's dark and sleek shop sits filled with stunning silver creations. Created by a highly trained team of western and Thai staff the studio works mainly with silver and precious gems to create synergies between the metal and stones. There is something for everyone in this contemporary store, elaborate designs as well as simple silver and gold bands. If you are not fully satisfied then the team can design a piece just for you and ship it to you at a later date. Alternatively Nova also offers a range of jewellery making courses for those wanting to create something for themselves.

www.nova-collection.com
Open: 9:00 -18:00
Address: 179 Thapae Road
Tel: +66 (0)53 273 058

METAL STUDIO THAILAND

A rising star in the jewellery world, Sirilak Samanasak is a Chiang Mai native who has been hand crafting her own pieces for the last 15 years. Finding her inspiration all over northern Thailand, Sirilak's creations are truly personal pieces from Chiang Mai. Her Studio in Nimmanhaemin road showcases a variety of metals, brass, silver and gold, precious and semi-precious stones and gems moulded into versatile and wearable pieces.

www.metal-studio-thailand.com
Open: 9:00 -20:00
Location: 28/2 Nimmanhaemin Road, Soi 11

ROYAL ORCHID COMPANY

An unusual set of jewellery creations, the Siam Royal Orchid Company have developed a technique of dipping real flowers, leaves, shells and seeds into clear lacquer, silver or gold to seal a little piece of nature within necklaces, bracelets and pendants. The signature pendant of ROC is the national symbol of Thailand – the orchid – which has been suspended in a lacquer pendant, as a way to retain the flowers beauty forever. Over the years the process of preservation has been refined and the orchid is now even available as a 24k gold version. The orchids are colourful, unique souvenirs from Thailand and each piece is truly individual. ROC has steadily been expanding the range to include roses, rice husks and even chili peppers encased in gold for those with a fiery personality. ROC has many stores throughout the city including within the Dhara Dhevi and Four Seasons resorts. Upon request they can also design bespoke pieces for special occasions.

www.royalorchidcollection.com
Open: 10:00 – 21:00
Location: Klang Wiang square, Behind Wawee coffee on Rachadamnoen Road

OTHER

HERB BASICS

One of the most popular pick and mix stores for quality spa and aromatherapy items, Herb Basics has cornered the market in Chiang Mai and is a great place to buy gifts for friends and family back home. Their products are made with locally sourced plants, herbs and essential oils and are made without chemicals. There are now seven different branches across the city, including two in Chiang Mai's international airport.

www.herbbasicschiangmai.com
Location: Klang Wieng Square, behind Wawee coffee, Ratchadamnoen Road
Open: Mon-Sat: 9.00 -18.00, Sun 14:00 022:00

GERARD COLLECTION

A small, specialist range of beautiful furniture can be found in the Gerard Collection. Located on the busy Nimmanhaemin Road the shop carries sofas, finely carved frames, chairs and cabinets made with a variety of different woods native to Thailand. Furniture may be too large to ship home, but the shop offers many smaller objects for home decoration that are easier to transport. If you enjoy the store then tours of their furniture factory are also available, just speak with the staff in the store for more information.

www.facebook.com/gerardcollection
Opening Hours: 10:00 - 17:00
Location: 6/23-24 Nimmanhaemin Road
Tel: +66(0)53 220604

CRAFITTI

A small white building with large tinted windows, even though it might look closed or empty, in reality behind the windows holds a shop full of beautiful, nature inspired pieces. The designs and details are delicate and there are some truly unique pieces from local designers working and living in Chiang Mai. Each piece is individually handmade and range from simple to elegant or elaborate, but there is something to match everyone's style.

Location: 173 Chareonraj Road
Open: Monday- Saturday 11:00 -19:00

SOP MOEI ARTS

A non profit organisation operating in Thailand for the last 30 years, Sop Moei Arts helps Karen and Pwo villagers in the Sop Moei district of northern Thailand to use their skills of weaving, basket making and textile designing to earn a basic income. As well as providing an essential income difficult to access in the remote villages, the program allows traditional skills to flourish. The store in Chiang Mai is located along the Ping river and stocks a range of unique, limited edition and one off products, including bags, baskets, table runners, cushions and mats. Their products are so unusual that they will be the talking piece of any home.

www.sopmoeiarts.com
Location:150/10 Chareonaj Road, Wat Gate
Open: 10:00 -19:00

SHINAWATRA THAI SILK

One of the largest silk producers in Thailand, the Shinawatra Thai Silk shops are owned by the famous political family of the same name. Their main shop on Huey Kaew Road holds a large range of silk and other local textiles, in a range of designs. There are also household items and clothing within the store and Shinawatra also offer made to order. Their shop is also a good place to learn about how silk is made and how the industry has evolved over the years.

www.shinawatrathaissilk.com

PAMPERING AND SPA TIME

Thailand is home to the Thai massage – a complex and invigorating treatment that relaxes the body and works out all the stress and knots in your body. Thai massages are known for their health properties as well as detoxifying, relaxing and strengthening benefits also. Add a country well versed in hospitality into the mix and you will find some of the best spas and the best range of pampering options. From head to foot massage, Chiang Mai boasts some of Thailand's finest spas, all at a fraction of the price in the West. While almost every luxury hotel has an accompanying spa, sometimes you just need a change of scenery and a visit to a different spa can make all the difference.

Anantara Spa lounge

ANANTARA SPA

Leading the way in luxury spas in Chiang Mai is the Anantara. A separate building within the grounds of the resort, many tourists come for a combination of spa treatments and high tea. Upon entering the spa, all five senses are greeted, from the smell of the herbs and treatment oils to the friendly welcome by the staff. Before the massage even begins, guests are lulled into a state of relaxation. As well as choosing the type of massage oil, guests are also offered a choice of music, pressure and focus points of the massage. The anantara spa has five individual treatment rooms, and five for couples, each with a herbal steam room and bathtub within the private sanctuary. The interior is decorated in a simple, zen style with wooden panels from floor to ceiling.

The Anantara Spa offers a whole range of individual treatments and packages to suit any guest. From A Detoxifying Chocolate Therapy To The Traditional Thai Massage Or An Elemis Pro-collagen Age Defy, There is a interesting range of treatments on offer. The signature of the Spa is the Lanna Ritual; a 90 minute pampering session that combines healing techniques of Thai, chinese and Burmese massage into a full body massage to improve energy flow and wellbeing. At the end of the treatment guests are woken up to a Tibetan singing bowl, wash any remaining negative energy away with floral water and offered a gold Bodhi leaf to hang in the neighbouring temple as a wish or prayer. Another signature spa treatment is the Essence of Anantara, a 200 minute spa session that offers foot reflexology, a Thai herbal steam, green tea scrub, oil massage and reflexology to beckon deep relaxation.

After finishing the pampering session, guests are offered tea and herbal cookies, leaving them to relax in the lounge and look out over the pool and riverside. There is no rush in the spa, and guests can sit as long as they want, until they are ready to continue their holiday.

www.chiang-mai.anantara.com/spas.aspx
Address: 123-123/1 Charoen Prathet Road, Chang Klan
Tel: +66 (0) 53 253 333

PANNA SPA

Hidden away and overlooking the rice fields of Siripanna Resort is the charming Panna Spa. Accessed by a wooden walkway hovering over a pond, entering Panna Spa makes you feel as if they have discovered a secret place. Upon entering you are greeted with a traditional wai from the staff, as well as the smell of lotus, jasmine and fresh flowers. A blanket of calmness envelopes guests as they sit in the dark teak lobby. While you choose your spa treatment and fill in the preference form, you are offered chilled rice tea to sip, freshly harvested from the rice fields.

The Panna Spa has nine private double and single rooms – perfect if you wish to either indulge yourself or if you want to have a couples pampering afternoon. The spa is open to visitors as well as guests staying in the hotel, and outside visitors will be rewarded with a tour of the Siripanna Resort as you walk to the spa. The most popular spa treatment is the Panna two hour Spa Buffet with a choice of one of 10 different treatments including Thai reflex body massage, Flora gems compress massage, an Oriental foot massage and even a post (golf) swing massage. Accompany your massage with two 30 minute treatments including a choice of Jasmine rice body scrub, Golden Rice body wrap, a Lanna Thai fresh herbal bath or an aromatic steam.

The Panna Spa also has a range of signature packages which range from 150-240 minutes. The Organic Garden Thai Therapy allows guests to be vitalized by the organic produce grown inside the Resort's grounds, and includes an organic banana rice scrub as well as an herbal steam, nourishing bath and 1.5 hour Thai reflexology massage. The Royal 9 Gems Golden Retreat is the ultimate in luxury and part ceremony, part spa experience. Based on your birth month, the corresponding gemstone will be used in the spa package, as well as a massage with gold infused massage oil and a royal gold facial. After four hours of golden pampering, you are sure to be as radiant as the sun.

www.pannaspa.com
Location: 36 Rat Uthit Road, Wat Ket
Tel: +66 (0) 5329 4656

THE SPA AT 137 PILLARS HOUSE

The Spa at 137 Pillars house is quite possibly Chiang Mai's best kept secret. A tiny but spectacularly designed building, The Spa features only four spa suites, including three singles and one double room, ideal for newlyweds. Upon entering the spa, you are welcomed by the aroma of essential oils, with hints of jasmine, frankincense and lavender, and then you are welcomed by the staff. While guests fill in a pre-treatment form, a welcome drink is offered, as is a chance to take in the beautiful interior. With white washed wood, plush adornments, and striped awnings, The Spa's décor immediately relaxes and transports guests to another realm. The exquisite ceiling mirror the stepping stones floating over the waterways outside, and a promise of what's to come lingers in the air.

The Spa has a thoughtful and varied menu of treatments for both men and women. Choose from facials and body scrubs to holistic and wellbeing treatments to realign your mind, body and soul. The jet lag recovery or immune recovery treatments are thoughtful answers to common problems. Traditional Thai massage, Luk Pra Kob herbal compress and the 90 minute Siamese combination offers guests a chance to try out different specialties of Thailand. For men, the exclusive package combines a body scrub, facial and hot oil massage to access energy caught in the deep tissue muscles. However, for the ultimate relaxation package visitors to the spa must try The Sukhothai Surrender. The 137 Pillars House's signature treatment, this two-hour relaxation journey combines traditional Thai massage, hot herbal compresses and Swedish massage techniques to leave guests floating out of the spa.

www.137pillarshouse.com
Address: 2 Soi 1, Nawatgate Road, Wat Gate
Tel: +66 (0) 53 247788

CHEEVA SPA

Cheeva Spa is a luxurious wellness spa offering massage packages, steams, sauna and body treatments such as scrubs and wraps. Cheeva means *the enjoyment of the happiness of life*. The spa has two branches in Chiang Mai and has won numerous awards over the years, including the TripAdvisor Certificate Of Excellence for highest rated spa four years in a row. Cheeva focuses on combining therapeutic and stress relieving treatments with traditional Lanna massage techniques to leave customers feeling relaxed and refreshed.

Cheeva Spa offers 12 different packages to choose from, ranging from two hours to four and a half. The Cheeva Experience Package includes a body scrub and body wrap, Lanna exotic massage, milky bath and a facial treatment. One of their most popular packages is the Cheeva Relax Package, which includes a traditional Thai massage, hot herbal compress and an aromatherapy oil massage. Masseuses are highly trained but are also allowed the freedom to adapt treatments to best suit individual customers. Both Cheeva Spa branches are decorated in traditional Thai style from the pillows to the chairs and play soothing music to relax customers.

The products used are as natural and organic as possible, favouring traditional herbs and locally sourced products where they can. There are even Thai herbal balls and herbal neck pillows available to take home and continue the Cheeva experience after your holiday. Upon booking, Cheeva Spa offers complimentary pick up and drop off services for customers from their hotels.

www.cheevaspa.com
Address: 4/2 Hussadhisawee Road
Phone: 053 405 129

THE OASIS SPA

Offering an impressive range of therapies, Oasis Spa uses the best of both international and traditional Asian techniques and products. This walled garden spa is in the centre of the old city and a true oasis in a busy city. The walls are decorated in warm terracotta and gold tones and inside the compound is a small shaded patio garden in front of the spa house, decorated in traditional Lanna style with a water feature to soothe your ears from the outside noise.

The staff at Oasis goes above and beyond to make your visit memorable and relaxing. From a pick and mix range of treatments to the ultimate indulging spa packages, there is something for everyone on their menu. The spa rooms are designed to fit two people to compliment their incredible four hands massage. Available for single guests, families, and couples on their honeymoon, the two therapists work in harmony as they perform a blissful oil massage and trigger relaxation points all across the body in tandem. Combine the four hand massage with a herbal steam, body scrub and clay full body wrap before the massage itself to fully release deep tensions in the Oasis Experience two hour package.

Oasis Spa Chiang Mai prides itself on using natural ingredients in many of their treatments. Products used for scrubs and wraps are freshly mixed for each customer using ingredients such a coconut, honey, aloe vera, and mint. Many of the herbs used are sourced from local villages around Chiang Mai, although a small percentage of their products, including essential oils, are imported from the renowned Biodroga range. Add to this well-trained masseurs and it is no surprise that Oasis Spa is one the most popular day spas in Chiang Mai. Oasis Spa's philosophy is to provide world-class treatments and they have succeeded.

www.oasisspa.net/destination/chiangmai
Address: 4 Samlan Road, Prasing, Muang, Chiang Mai 50200
Tel: +66 53 920 111

FAH LANNA SPA

The high, white-washed walls and plants that border Fah Lanna Spa in Chiang Mai's Old Town give you a hint of their philosophy: keeping all the noise and stress of the city outside this calming spa. Offering a variety of traditional Thai and oil massages as well as a cafe with a picturesque water garden, half a day can easily be spent at Fah Lanna Spa enjoying the relaxing treatments and forgetting the rest of the world exists. As the sign outside the spa says, this place is "easy to find, hard to forget".

Fah Lanna Spa has two locations, but the one in the old city offers a far more luxurious experience. The Spa is in the heart of the old city, hidden along a quiet road and they offer a free shuttle to pick guests up in style. With an ornate wooden entrance and a small bridge leading into the cozy reception guests are welcomed with herbal tea and arm chairs to melt into. From here, you can enjoy the view of the long wooden walkway stretching the length of the fish pond, fringed by bamboo and ferns while you choose your treatments.

The treatment rooms and facilities are just as exquisite, combining natural elements with subtle touches of Lanna décor. Both the single and couples' rooms come with an in-suite shower and bathroom, but if you are considering a package then you may also wish to enjoy the in-room Jacuzzi. There is also a rather unusual herbal steam cave, where you can enjoy herbal scents which deeply cleanse your skin. Fah Lanna Spa offers a series of beauty treatments including body scrubs, facials, waxing, manicures, and pedicures. If you are looking for some serious pampering then consider their packages, which can last between two and five hours. For a typical Chiang Mai experience try the Fah Lanna Northern Style, which is a two hour treatment that includes reflexology, Thai massage and Tok Sen. The Fah Lanna Nirvana is the full five-hour package that allows you to enjoy everything, starting with an aromatic herbal steam, then a body scrub, wrap, aromatherapy oil massage using a scent of your choice and ending with a facial treatment.

www.fahlanna.com
Address: 57/1 Wiang Kaew Road, near corner of Jabhan Road
Tel: +66 (0) 53 416191

KIYORA SPA

Kiyora Spa is one of the most popular spa and wellness centres in Chiang Mai, and they offer a range of massages, spa and beauty treatments, a sauna and swimming pool, and couples treatments for customers who wish to pamper themselves while on honeymoon. Most of the treatments are based on traditional Thai methods and include the use of special medicinal herbs for relaxation, energizing or healing. One of the most popular packages is Thai Inspired, which includes a traditional Thai massage, foot reflexology, and the use of a heated herbal compress over the course of two and a half hours. There is also a four and a half hour Spa-Vacation package, which starts with a scrub and wrap before a deep tissue Swedish massage and Glow facial, to leave guests refreshed and renewed on their holiday.

At the end of each spa package, guests are given complimentary mango and sticky rice, as well as herbal tea. Kiyora Spa also offers free pick up and drop off for customers within Chiang Mai city which is useful if you don't know the city well. It's useful to know that they offer discounts when you book online at their website.

www.kiyoraspa.com
Opening Hours: 10:00 - 22:00
Address: 26/1 Chang Moi Road, Soi 2, Chiang Mai
Tel: +66 (0) 52 003 268

DHEVA SPA AND WELLNESS CENTRE

One of the largest and most luxurious spas in Chiang Mai, a visit to the Dheva Spa and Wellness centre allows you to also experience the full glory of the Dhara Dhevi Resort, as well as get pampered in a palace. The Dheva Spa took over three years to build and was expertly designed by a team of 150 artists in Chiang Mai to fully represent an auspicious Buddhist temple in Mandalay, Myanmar. Each of the 11 different treatment rooms features a private bath, heated marble scrub table, and a relaxation area.

The menu of treatments is as remarkable as the spa itself, with close to 100 different treatments. As well as traditional Thai treatments, Dheva Spa also focuses on Ayurvedic treatments to balance the body, and expert specialists can guide you from defining your dosha to preparing a personalized Ayurvedic program of treatments to balance your body.

If Ayurveda sounds too new age hippie for you, then Dheva Spa has countless other treatments available, sourced from all across the world. Play it safe and try the luxurious indulgence package, which features aromatherapy massage and a personalized facial treatment. Transport yourself to Northern Africa and enjoy a Rasul – a blend of mineral rich mud, steam and heat to release toxins and smooth dry skin. If you have been over indulging on your holiday then try the traditional Chinese Qi Nei Zang abdominal massage to release emotional tension, cleanse your intestines and assist in the detoxification process. As well as spa treatments the Dheva Spa also offers hairdressing, manicures, a hydrotherapy room and Vichy shower, yoga and meditation classes and even a Watsu pool.

www.dharadhevi.com/EN/Spa-Wellness
Location: 51/4 Chiang Mai - Sankampaeng Road, Moo 1
Tel: +66 (0) 53 888 888

RARINJINDA WELLNESS SPA

Rarinjinda Wellness Spa is part of a beautiful resort near the Ping River offering lots of different luxury treatments. Despite being located in the middle of Chiang Mai city, the spa is quiet and relaxing, making guests feel like they are they are far from the city in a secluded place of sheer tranquility. Rarinjinda Wellness Spa has a menu offering traditional and oil massages, a detox sauna or steam, herbal hot compresses and body scrubs. The spa packages range in time and price with the longest package (Golden Memories, which includes Guava Foot Polisher, Siamese Herbal Steam, body mask, Jacuzzi therapy and a Shirodhara Treatment) taking five hours.

Rarinjinda Wellness Spa has a range of Hydro therapies not found elsewhere in Chiang Mai, as well as a large hydro pool with a Jacuzzi. The Sandy & Splashy Vichy Massage includes exfoliation and a water massage. Rarinjinda Wellness Spa is popular among tourists and the Spa has a limit on the maximum number of guests at any one time so booking ahead is advised. A complimentary pick up service is available for those who book in advance.

www.rarinjinda.com
Address: 14 Charoenraj Road, Wat Ket
Tel: +66 (0) 53 303 030

WHERE TO NEXT? TRIPS OUT OF CHIANG MAI

Chiang Mai is the perfect base for exploring Northern Thailand. From its small but well connected airport, to the winding mountainous roads leading to adventures in all directions, it is a good idea to get out of Chiang Mai at some point while visiting. In every direction, there is something amazing and unique, yet Thailand excels at its hidden beauty accessible to those who want to see it. Most of the north is accessible by car (although it's recommended to hire a driver to reduce the stress of driving in Thailand), attractions are well signposted in English and in emergencies, there are phone and 3g connections in most areas – so you'll only get lost if you want to!

CHIANG RAI

For those who find Chiang Mai too busy, Chiang Rai will be much more relaxing and manageable. A sleepier and more traditional Thai city, Chiang Rai was founded about 30 years before Chiang Mai by the same King, and at the time was the capital of the Mengrai Kingdom (later known as the Lanna Kingdom). Chiang Rai is not as touristic as its big sister Chiang Mai, but it can be argued that as a city it is even more important, thanks to its more temperate climate, the rich valley with the beautiful Mae Kok River, and close proximity to Myanmar (the border is less than an hour north), Laos and South Western China – also known as the Golden Triangle area.

Chiang Rai has a similar history as the rest of the North, with frequent invasions from its neighbours, and in fact was under Burmese rule for hundreds of years before rejoining the Lanna Kingdom and then Siam. However, due to its turbulent past, the region of Chiang Rai province holds more ethnic groups (the Karen, Akha, Lisu, Meo, and Hmong) and hill tribes than any other province in Thailand.

The surrounding area is quite mountainous, and there are plenty of opportunities to visit coffee plantations, elephants centres, remote hill tribe villages and the magnificent Wat Rong Khun, the White temple. There is also the lesser known Baan Dam museum, known as the black temple, which was created by the national artist Thawan Duchanee and includes a mixture of 40 black houses, filled with art, sculptures, animal bones and skins. It is an odd place but for those into art, it's definitely worth a visit.

MAE SAI & GOLDEN TRIANGLE

From Chiang Rai, an interesting day trip is to the Burmese border town of Mae Sai, where tourists can cross over into the small, trading town of Tachileik. Carrying on along the border, you can visit the Golden Triangle and take a boat across into Laos (visa free but with the requirement that you return across the river by sundown). There is even a large casino complex where the three borders meet, although it's often mixed up with narcotics smuggling and so it's advised only the brave (or foolish) visit.

DOI TUNG ROYAL VILLA

Being far north and mountainous, this region is cooler than most, especially during winter months (November to February), which is one reason the Doi Tung Royal Villa was constructed in the area. The Royal Villa was built from Princess Srinagarindra's private fund, as she wanted to start the Doi Tung Development Project in the area. The development project involves reforestation, improving the livelihood of local hill tribe people and increasing sustainable development in the region, as well as encouraging opium farmers to cultivate new crops such as coffee and macadamia nuts. The Royal Villa was built with discarded teak trees and recycled pine wood, and the interior radiates simplicity, elegance and functionality, just as the King's mother did.

The villa is open daily for tours, and be sure to pay close attention to the hand crafted ceiling of the main hall. Designed by the Astronomy Society of Thailand, there are little bulbs representing the stars showing the position of the constellations on October 21, 1900, the day the Princess Mother was born.

MAE FAH LUANG GARDEN

Near the Royal Villa is the impressive Mae Fah Luang gardens. Originally an Akha village that was an important stop on the opium route, it has now been turned into a colourful paradise allowing Thais to view a temperate flower garden without having to travel abroad.

CHIANG RAI RESORTS

Most of Chiang Rai province can be seen in 3 days, and there are also some beautiful hotels to stay in, most offering stunning views overlooking rice paddies and mountain ranges. A few to consider are:

Manee Dheva Resort – elegant stand alone villas surrounded by rice paddies and reached by raised walkways.

www.maneedhevaresort.com/en/

Katiliya Mountain Resort & Spa – Nestled in the misty hills near the Golden Triangle, the resort offers priceless views of the surrounding valley and lakes, a full spa and spacious halls available for wedding parties.

www.katiliya.com/chiangrai/

GOLDEN TRIANGLE ELEPHANT CAMPS

Visiting one of the two tented camps in Chiang Rai is possibly the most luxurious thing you can do North of Bangkok and is a once in a lifetime experience. At first I researched into which hotel copied the idea from the other, but as it turns out, both hotel brands are owned by the same parent group, so the quality will be similar for both. The major difference is whether you wish to stay in a hotel or a tent. And when I say tent I mean a luxurious, 5-star tent with Wi-Fi, a real bed, and a freestanding bath tub.

ANANTARA CHIANG RAI

A stylish resort spread across more than 150 acres of lush forest and overlooking the Mekong river, The Anantara Chiang Rai resort has 77 rooms, two restaurants, squash courts, one spa, and 25 elephants for neighbours. The spectacular infinity pool is reason enough to stay at Anantara, as well as the Mahout training camp. Part of the Anantara resort houses a traditional mahout village, which works alongside the Golden Triangle Asian Elephant Foundation to offer guests a chance to meet and learn the skills of elephant guiding.

Established in 2003, the Golden Triangle Asian Elephant Foundation has tirelessly performed street rescues, provided employment and a comfortable lifestyle for the elephants and their entire mahout families, and participated in bigger picture projects for the gentle giant. They now support more than 25 elephants and 60 people, and are proudly fully funded by Anantara Hotels, Resorts & Spas, the Minor parent company and guest donations.

www.goldentriangle.anantara.com

FOUR SEASONS TENTED CAMP

While you can find 5-star luxury and experienced elephants in Chiang Mai, you will rarely get a chance to stay in a Four Seasons tented camp (except maybe in Africa), or one that also has a wine cellar! Standing alone and spread out on a forested hillside in the middle of the rainforest, the 15 air conditioned tents are connected by a brick lined bamboo path. Inside the spacious tents are ornate writing desks, hardwood floors, an ornate bathtub, outdoor deck with a hot tub, and countless other small details that will make this stay unforgettable. Take a bath with the elephants at sunset, or watch them stroll to their morning drink at the river over breakfast. The Four Seasons Tented Camp can custom make tours to suit whatever you are looking for on your holiday. They also specialise in wedding and honeymoon packages (see www.fourseasons.com/goldentriangle/weddings/ for more details).

The Four Seasons shares the same elephants as the Anantara, so regardless of which camp you visit, part of your money goes to supporting the Golden Triangle Asian Elephant Foundation. To experience elephants up close and personal and to take the time to learn about how to properly care for them is a privilege and a unique experience to Northern Thailand.

PAI

Pai is a quaint, hippie town with a relaxed vibe about 80 km from Chiang Mai, and sitting in a valley surrounded by mountains. Most tourists who visit Chiang Mai also go to Pai instead of Chiang Rai because of the fact that it is not a city, rather merely a small town that became popular with travellers through word of mouth. There are only two ways to get there, by road or by air. The flight is under 30 minutes and offers birds eye mountain views. Over the years the city has become more busy, but the quality on offer has also improved, new restaurants and an interesting walking street has opened and there are now two 5-star resorts on the outskirts of town.

REVERIE SIAM

A great example of Thai's perfecting vintage style, the Reverie Siam is a delight to stay at. With two outdoor pools, vistas of the mountains and Pai River, and a choice of 20 uniquely decorated rooms, this hotel will allow you to experience a bygone era.

www.reveriesiam.com

PAI ISLAND RESORT

A small boutique hotel with only 10 villas, each designed by celebrated Thai artists, the villas are each uniquely decorated and allow guests to relax into Pai island life. Only 5 minutes from the city centre, the resort is surrounded by manicured gardens. Each villa has its own outdoor shower and bathtub allowing guests to really experience nature.

www.paiislandresort.com

MONTIS RESORT

Montis Resort offers rustic luxury for adventurers and as well as beautiful safari inspired rooms, they also offer a whole range of activities, from whitewater rafting and archery to treks to hill tribes and onsite they have a heated swimming pool for the cool winter months.

www.montisresort.com

CHIANG DAO

A beautiful small town incorporated into the stunning nature of Northern Thailand, Chiang Dao is a haven for nature lovers, honeymooners and those looking to escape all aspects of city life. The name translates roughly into 'city of stars' and at night the sky is so clear that all the stars are visible. The area is famous for the five interconnected caves that stretch for many kilometres, with two of the caves open to the public to see natural formations and buddhist carvings added to the interior. The magnificent Doi Chiang Dao mountain sits in the backdrop of the sleepy little town, and is Thailand's third highest mountain at 2,225 metres (and walkable for those who enjoy hiking) and home to a variety of rare bird species. It's also an ideal base for those wishing to tour the area, by car, motorbike or bicycle, and the Elephant Nature Park, as well as lots of adventurous activities like water rafting and trekking are available nearby.

CHIANG DAO NEST

An amazing little resort that has expanded into two locations. The Nest 1 is a cozy resort including 20 bamboo huts with luxurious interiors and a small pool. The Nest 2 is more spacious and has some impressive views of the mountains, as well as a few comfortable hammocks. Both locations have amazing restaurants, with the Nest 1's kitchen being world famous and specialising in Western and European cuisine, while the Nest 2 has an impressive Thai menu.

www.chiangdaonest.com
Tel: +66 (0) 53 456 612
Email: nest@chiangdao.com

AZALEA VILLAGE

A relatively unknown resort with a beautiful pool and amazing views of Doi Chiang Dao. Azalea Village has 21 different cottages which blend simplicity, luxury and nature together to create an atmosphere of serenity. The resort is surrounded in nature and the perfect base to explore the surroundings of Northern Thailand, or to stay put and read a book (or five).

www.azalea-village.com
Tel: +66 (0) 53-456-168
Email: reservation@azalea-village.com

MOUNTAIN FLOAT

Imagine a villa on a lake, where you can step right off the living area into the water. A beautiful, natural setting with wooden rooms constructed in elegant styles. The finish and fine details of the resort leave you feeling like you've entered a natural wonderland. Mountain Float resort rests on Mae Ngat Dam about an hour north of Chiang Mai and in the heart of Sri Lanna National Park. Mornings on the deck are cool and peaceful, with mist encircling the nearby mountains, while even in the heat of the day the water remains cool. Mountain Float has a range of fun water toys to play with, from trampolines and canoes to a solo sailboat for those who wish to explore the lake further. Mountain Float organises everything for guests, from the boat to breakfast, although other meals are separate but can be ordered at the resort restaurant. It's advisable to book early as Mountain Float fills up quickly and the smallest 'sunday' houseboat fits 4 people (but couples can book both rooms and just stay alone), while the largest fits up to 20 people and is an amazing place to spend your honeymoon.

www.mountainfloat.net
Tel: +66 (0)93 615 6365
E-mail: infomountainfloat@gmail.com

SUKHOTHAI HISTORICAL PARK

Sukhothai is a UNESCO world heritage site and Thailand's version of Angkor Wat. The official first capital of Siam during the 13th century, all that remains of old Sukhothai are numerous historical sites, the ancient city ruins, as well as the seemingly lavish temples and monuments to Buddhism. The name Sukhothai means the 'dawn of happiness' and as the name suggests, the ancient city is best explored at dawn (or sunset).

The Historical Park holds 193 ruins and covers over 70 square kilometres of land. Within these city walls, which are defined by a moat just like Chiang Mai, various kings have ruled the country, the Thai alphabet was created, the monarchy and governments were intertwined and Siam's boundaries were expanded from careful planning. There is so much history within the ancient capital and it is recommended to hire a guide for the day, as well as bicycles to cover the vast area of ruins. Sukhothai is a wonderful alternative to Angkor Wat and much less crowded, allowing visitors a chance to really absorb the atmosphere of the capital of an ancient kingdom.

Most travellers will visit Sukhothai in a day (a four-hour drive from Chiang Mai), but history lovers might prefer to stay overnight and explore at sunrise. While there are no 5-star hotels in the area, Sukhothai Heritage resort by the Unique collection and Legendha Sukhothai resorts are good 4-star options.

EVENTS

Chiang Mai celebrates national holidays in style, thanks to its cultural and artistic heritage, and the city attracts both international and domestic tourists for major events. Being such a beautiful city, Thai's as well as foreigners flock to the city to celebrate Loy Kratong and Songkran (Thai new year), and it is wise to schedule holidays around these events to see the amazing festivals and the festivities that occur for them. In addition to the countrywide festivals, Chiang Mai also has smaller and ancient Lanna inspired festivals, such as Yee Ping, the Bo Sang Umbrella festival and even a city wide flower festival.

JANUARY

BOR SANG UMBRELLA FESTIVAL

Location: Bor Sang Village, Sankhampaeng District

Occurring mid January every year, this festival has expanded from a small village fair to a well known festival. Located a little south of the city in Bor Sang village, this colourful festival lasts three days and includes parades of beautiful handcrafted parasols with vivid motifs made from silk or fine mulberry paper. The otherwise sleepy town is transformed into an artistic haven, handicraft exhibits, street fairs and cultural performances, and a parade featuring the winner of the Miss Bor Sang beauty pageant.

CHINESE NEW YEAR

Location: Warorot Market (Kad Luang), Chiang Mai

Falling at the end of January or early February (depending on the Lunar calendar), Chinese new year brings festivities but also lots of crowds. Around the Chinese area of Warorot market there are daily festivities, dances, a fire dragon show and exhibitions from Chinese artists as well as the history of the Chinese community in Thailand.

FEBUARY

CHIANG MAI FLOWER FESTIVAL

Location: Suan Bok Haad, Narawat Bridge & Arak Road

The Flower festival is a colourful and aromatic display for all the senses. The festival revolves around a parade route around the old city featuring exquisite floral sculptures balanced on detailed floats which tour the city centre in the early evening. The parade floats are shaped to look like temples, animals, and occasionally an elaborate scene from a Thai legend.

If you are a flower enthusiast, watch out for the rare Damask rose, local to Chiang Mai province. While the dates change yearly for the flower festival, most of the activities are always around Suan Haad Park in the southwest corner of the old city. Combine this with a trip to the Royal Flora Ratchaphruek botanical gardens, which has an impressive variety of Southeast Asian and European flowers on display.

MAKHA BUCHA DAY

Location: Buddhist Temples throughout the country

An important date on the Buddhist calendar during the full moon of the third lunar month, Makha Bucha Day celebrates a spontaneous sermon the Buddha gave to over one thousand disciples who all eventually became enlightened. The ceremony involves circling stupas and Buddhist prayer halls with candles and incense, visiting temples donating alms to monks and observing the five Buddhist precepts for wholesome living. Travellers are welcome to watch ceremonies and may be invited to join in, but remember to wear white and cover knees and shoulders to be respectful.

STRAWBERRY FAIR

Location: throughout Samoeng District

When the strawberries are ripe and ready, the small town of Samoeng – a 30 minute drive from Chiang Mai – throws a fair to celebrate. Strawberries are difficult to grow in Thailand's tropical conditions and Samoeng is proud of its farmers and fields. The town puts on a parade, beauty contest, a cycling event and many other fruit related events. There are also lots of stalls selling strawberries by the kilo, strawberry smoothies and cake baking contests. The atmosphere is fun and upbeat and a surprising amount of people visit the fair from all over the country.

APRIL

SONGKRAN (THAI NEW YEAR)

Location: Nationwide

Songkran is the Thai name for the Buddhist New Year festival, which is celebrated across Southeast Asia. Thailand is well known internationally for the festival, which involves a nationwide three-day water fight. The festival is to mark the coming of the rains, the end of the year and a chance for a fresh start, and what better way to wash off your sins than with water! All across the city, people spend the three days outside, spraying and splashing each other using water guns, buckets and anything else that can hold and launch water.

Chiang Mai is hailed for being the best city to experience Songkran in due to the old city's moat – an easily accessible source of water. Traffic around this festival is at a standstill but it is an astounding sight to see. It is also virtually impossible to leave your hotel without getting wet so if you plan on being in Thailand around mid-April factor in Songkran, for the whole country shuts down to play in this festival. Thanks to the hot weather in April, the water becomes a refreshing cool down. The festival falls around the 13th April, but depends on exact lunar dates to decide the days where water is thrown.

MAY

WISAKHA BUCHA DAY

Location: Buddhist temples across the country

The most important day in the Buddhist calendar, Wisakha Bucha Day marks the Buddha's birthday, day of his death, and the day of his enlightenment. The exact date depends on the full moon of the sixth month, but usually falls towards the end of May. This is a beautiful holiday with families and individuals all going to pay respect at their local temple. In the evening, there is a candlelight procession and chanting at larger temples offered by the monks. Participants should walk around the main shrine three times, to signify each important day in Buddha's life: the triple jewel of Buddhism.

In Chiang Mai, Wisakha Bucha day is celebrated the evening before with thousands of people walking up the road to Wat Doi Suthep after sunset (to arrive before midnight at the temple). There is food and drink along the road leading to the temple and the atmosphere of thousands of people on a pilgrimage is electrifying - this energy helps you forget you are walking up a small mountain.

NOVEMBER

YEE PING

Yee (or Yi) Peng Festival is Chiang Mai's most well known festival, thanks to the 2012 Lonely Planet cover highlighting the festival). It's a truly incredible event to be part of and if the Songkran water fight doesn't appeal, then this one will. The exact date varies wildly every year and isn't officially set until two months before November, lanterns are also let off on the full moon of the twelfth month (the same date as Loy Kratong – the holiday that it is part of) but the arranged ceremonies usually occurs a week before Loy Kratong madness. Yee Peng involves people releasing thousands of sky lanterns into the night sky, releasing bad luck and letting go of misfortunes. Fiery lanterns rise up all across the night sky over Chiang Mai and with them wishes for new beginnings and better luck rise with them. Buddhists also believe that if you make a wish when you set off the lantern, it will come true if you do good deeds the following year. As well as the lanterns, there are Thai dance shows, parades (yes, Chiang Mai loves parades), live music at Thapae gate and many other festivities to celebrate Yee Ping (and Loy Kratong).

While lanterns are lit off everywhere, the official (and magical) event occurs in Mae Jo University with a Buddhist ceremony followed by a group release. Because of the popularity and bad behaviour from tourists in 2015 the local authorities started charging for the previously free event. The official release is more than worth the cover charge, but don't be confused with another Yee Ping festival set up for tourists – the tourist one is usually held after Loy Kratong, while the genuine one is on the full moon date. Both are unique ceremonies and will give you spectacular pictures and beautiful memories, but the original one is organised by a temple so you will need to dress in white for the event.

LOY KRATONG

Loy Kratong is called one of Thailand's most romantic celebrations. Imagine hundreds of small 'boats' with candles, offerings to the spirits and flowers, floating along rivers and waterways, while sky lanterns light the night sky. In Thai the word 'loy' means to float and 'kratong' means a small raft, which explains the festival perfectly. The rafts are made of banana trunk and elaborately folded leaves, decorated with flowers and incense sticks. Some people also add hair or nail clippings, so the spirits know who sent the Kratong, and usually coins are also stowed on the raft as way of sharing wealth (with many hoping by giving more will come back to them).

The festival was traditionally the practice of sending gifts to the serpent ruler of water to stop the rain and leave the rivers alone to run tranquility. Nowadays, the festival symbolizes letting go of grudges, problems and anger, to start life afresh, with the kratong as an offering to pardon any past sins. While Loy Kratong happens nationwide, Chiang Mai is one of the nicest places to celebrate due to the various bodies of water around the city. As well as the actual festival there are activities throughout the city, including Loy Krathong contests, firework displays and boat races on the ping river. November is said to be the best time for Loy Kratong as the rivers are at their fullest and the full moon is at its brightest in the clear night sky.

DECEMBER

CHRISTMAS & NEW YEAR

Both Christian holidays are celebrated in Thailand, with most hotels and restaurants offering Christmas Day dinners or New Years parties, but the meaning for Thai natives is not the same, and most of the country continues as normal across these two major western holidays. However, many places recognize it is the busiest tourist season and so if you are planning on visiting over Christmas, then it is wise to book well in advance. And once the New Year signs go up, they stay up until April. So technically New Year lasts four months in Thailand.

PRACTICAL ISSUES

Now that you know where you want to eat, sleep and explore, there are a few practical issues you need to think about before your perfect holiday begins.

WEATHER

Thailand can be hot, humid and rainy but it can also be sunny, fresh and cool with Chiang Mai boasting the best weather of the country, depending on the time of the year. The best time to visit Northern Thailand is between November – January as the temperatures are cool in the evenings, moderate in the day time and the sky is almost always blue, except for a few fluffy white clouds. November – January is also Thailand's peak tourist season, with Loy Kratong, Yee Ping, Christmas and western New Year all falling in that time period.

While November to January boasts ideal weather, in late February the temperatures start rising and in March, along with 40°C weather, the local farmers burn the fields creating a terrible blanket of pollution over the city. While this is the worst time to travel, it is definite tourist low season and so you can score some great deals on hotels and upgrades, as well as having the infinity pools to yourselves.

April is classified as high season again because of the Songkran holiday, but since Songkran is a celebration trying to bring the rains, as soon as the festivities are over the monsoon season begins. May to August usually brings daily rains and the occasional storm, but Chiang Mai doesn't suffer from monsoons the way the rest of Asia seems to. Rainy season in Chiang Mai usually means a few hours of rain a day and before the rain, a giant rain cloud making its way across the sky, signaling you to get indoors. Rainy season in Chiang Mai can be quite pleasant (as long as you are not driving a motorbike when it starts to rain), with the rain leaving fresh, cool temperatures and Doi Pui mountain glowing a bright green.

September and October are usually overlooked as the best months of the year because nothing much happens in terms of festivals, and occasionally the rain can continue through parts of September. However, overall they are pleasant and not as crowded as the high season, and with the new influx of Chinese tourists to Chiang Mai in the last few years the city is much more enjoyable when it is not high season!

Months	Season
November-January	Cool
February-April	Hot (and smoky)
May-August	Rainy
September-October	Slightly rainy/cool

VISAS

For most countries getting to Thailand was easy, and the government offers 30 or 90 day visas on arrival at the airport for free*. If you wish to spend longer than 30 days in Thailand, then it is worth buying a visa in advance at a Thai embassy outside of the country – you can get a single 60 day visa or a double entry (60 x 2). However, if you have a double entry (or no visa and wish to stay longer than your 30 day visa on arrival) then Thailand simply requires you to leave and re-enter the country to either activate the second visa or get another 30 day stamp. If you plan on a longer holiday, then it makes sense to visit one of Thailand's neighbors halfway through your trip (such as Myanmar, Cambodia and Angkor Wat, or even Vietnam or Malaysia) to ensure your visa covers your whole stay.

If you are a frequent visitor to Thailand for business, pleasure, or you just hate to wait in immigration lines then there is a special visa called the elite visa which allows you to bypass all airport security and immigration and travel in style. The visa lasts for 5 years and isn't cheap (individual membership starts at 500,000 Baht) but for some repeat travelers it might be worth it. See www.thailandelite.com for more details.

*If you often need visas to travel (such as Ukrainian or Ugandan passports), then it is worth checking www.thaiembassy.org/main/ in advance to see your specific visa requirements.

AIRPORT LOUNGES

Chiang Mai's airport is small and compact, but very central and easy to navigate. There are three small lounges – two Thai airways lounges gate side and a mediocre Bangkok airways lounge before check in. Since CNX is pretty small and comfortable, there is no need to check into a lounge unless you are looking for extra privacy.

However, Bangkok is a different story. Bangkok's Suvarnabhumi airport transfers close to 50 Million people yearly, but it is not a place you want to hunt for a seat in. While the airport flows well, it is always busy and if you are looking to escape the holiday makers it's advisable to check into one of its 6 airport lounges. Free with a priority pass or if you fly first class with most airlines, but you can also book online for a 2/3/5 hour visit (usually $50) or pay at the door, assuming they aren't busy.

MEDICAL AND SAFETY ISSUES

Thailand is a very safe place if you aren't looking for drugs or prostitution and petty theft is the only serious thing to look out for. Health insurance is essential for travel in Thailand, just in case of emergency. Make sure your insurance covers you for elephant riding (or motorbikes if you plan on exploring the roads). However, generally Thailand is a safe and clean country and most likely the problems will come from traffic accidents, mosquitoes or occasional food poisoning. But even all three of these are unlikely if you wear mosquito repellent, don't eat at questionable restaurants or drive over 100 miles an hour (or drive at all).

When it comes to mosquitoes there is not much point taking anti-malarial medicine as it doesn't stop you from getting bit. Rather, just ensure that you spray repellent around sunrise, sunset and in the evenings. Chiang Mai has a few different hospitals but by far the best one is Chiang Mai Ram, located on the west side of the moat. All the doctors at Ram speak perfect English, and almost all have received part of their medical training abroad. For absolute emergencies, Chiang Mai Ram also has a helipad on the roof and Northern Thailand has an active group of Sky Doctors to come to the rescue in remote areas. For travel insurance World Nomads offers great coverage that can be bought and activated on the same day.

MONEY

Thailand uses Thai Baht and currency exchanges welcome all major currencies equally. Credit cards are accepted in all major hotels and are advisable over bringing lots of cash, but there are also cash points that pay out in Baht accept major cards all over the country. However traveler's cheques are a nightmare to cash, as most people don't understand what to do with them.

THE END

Thank you for purchasing Luxurious Chiang Mai and I hope you managed to plan your dream getaway with it. I would love to know your thoughts about the guide, so if you could leave me an Amazon review that would be incredibly useful for advertising the guide. And if you want to connect with me, or get the latest updates from Chiang Mai the check out the following:

Website: www.luxurychiangmai.com

Facebook: www.facebook.com/luxurychiangmai

Instagram: www.instagram.com/luxury_chiang_mai

Made in the USA
Monee, IL
21 November 2022